INSPIRE YOUR

MARRIAGE

by John Thomas.

ISBN 978-1-7364357-0-0.

For questions, go to www.InspireYourMarriage.com.

Contents

Section One

Keeping The Spark Alive

Truly eye-opening! Reading, talking and learning about relationships, as well as self-development, has been my passion for a long time. What I've learned from other couples about what made their relationship work, including what makes them feel good about themselves, was eye-opening and really unexpected.

Their stories listed in this book are part relationship advice, part self-help advice. They revitalized their marriage, rejuvenated their libido and they individually felt better than they had in a long time. Each of their revelations were different, but they all had one thing in common.

Chapter 1

(Re) Igniting The Connection

Actions Create Reactions

For a long time, they couldn't figure it out. "We will be doing good for a while, then something will derail us," Morgan and Hayden admitted. Sometimes they would feel really close to each other, other times they felt miles away. Over the years they simply drifted apart and were not feeling as connected. Their intimacy wasn't dead, but it certainly wasn't as passionate as it used to be.

Just when they thought it was hopeless, they started recognizing that certain behaviors triggered unusually positive responses in each other. Their daily actions, including what they did for themselves, would generate a warm sexy feeling from their spouse toward them, often automatically without conscious thought.

What shocked them though was that the things that generated the best responses in their spouse weren't things that would generate the same positive response in themselves if their spouse did them. They began to understand they reacted to things differently and not to minimize what each of them finds appealing.

The second surprising result was that when Morgan did something that Hayden found appealing, Hayden often responded with an action or behavior that Morgan found appealing. And vice versa. They didn't realize the power they each had to get their spouse to happily do what was meaningful to them.

They had somehow stumbled upon a secret that changed their marriage. It seemed so easy, yet so foreign. Their passion for each other is again like when they first met, both in and out of the bedroom. Their attraction to each other is out of this world. Their love, spark and connection have all been reignited.

What was the secret? Their actions created reactions in their spouse. When they actively show qualities their spouse finds attractive, through their behavior and words, their spouse instinctively and reactively shows qualities they find attractive. But the real difference maker was understanding which things affected each of them the most and how to effectively display those qualities.

When dating, they fell in love because they both displayed qualities that the other person was attracted to. But over time, some of those things weren't as evident as they once were. Re-discovering those qualities and uncovering new ones not only improved the marriage, but they individually felt happier.

Pulling Closer or Pushing Away

Relationships seem like they should be easy! Find someone you like; date for a while to establish a connection; seal the deal with a life-long commitment. Simple, right? What we forget to recognize is the actual simple part – A person's continued actions, behavior and words either pulls their spouse closer to them or inadvertently pushes their spouse away.

For you, the key is to truly understand which qualities you and your spouse find most attractive in each other, even the little things that are easy to overlook, that would get you to respond positively back to each other. That's the aim of this – get clues for you to discover those little things, as well as actions to be taken for you both to display those things to one another.

It's not just that each of you find certain qualities attractive, it's that those things are important to each of you and vital to feeling close. When you do what's important to your spouse, it makes them happy. When they're happy, they're inspired to reciprocate with what makes you happy. Doing what genuinely makes them happy benefits you too!

It's a mindset shift. Instead of focusing on what should or should not be done in marriage, it's a focus on doing what's important to each other. If something is important to your spouse, do it even if you normally wouldn't. But make sure they're doing what's important to you also. It's a win/win for both of you.

Based on this concept, hear couples revealing their stories and learn what was important to them for turning their marriage around to be dynamic again. These are real solutions for you to make your own marriage transformation, even if it's just a small tweak to make a good marriage be just a little better.

The bonus is that you can also focus on your own mental health self-care with healthy self-esteem tips, anxiety control and other personal self-help issues. It's relationship advice for communication skills, better connection and passionate chemistry, but it's so much more than that!

The Blend of Independent and Team Qualities

The key aspect for the spark is that we need to feel united with our spouse without losing each other's autonomy. People are attracted to both the individuality in their spouse, known as their "Independent" qualities; and to the flexibility in their spouse, their "Team" qualities. Displaying both sides to each other creates a well-balanced ideal.

The "Independent" qualities show how people view and treat themselves. We are attracted to our spouse when they are driven in their own life and have some sense of self-focused autonomy. We admire and appreciate it when they are not hesitant to show who they are as a person.

The "Team" qualities show how people view and treat others, especially their spouse. We are attracted to our spouse when they show they adore us and are crazy about us in a way we can truly feel it. We admire and appreciate it when they show flexibility and kindness to care about fulfilling our desires and to cherish us.

The amazing thing is that when you combine these two types of qualities, you can see positive results immediately! This is not a long, drawn out process trying to do a major overhaul. It's easy, succinct and simple to implement.

Pinpoint the one Independent quality and one Team quality that your spouse is instinctively drawn to and the two qualities that you're instinctively drawn to. Then inspire your spouse to do those things that make you feel close and important to you by doing the things that make them feel close and important to them. And them doing the same for you. It becomes a positive feedback loop instead of a negative one.

This will help the marriage, your sex life and even your own mental health!

The Independent Qualities

Show your interesting, self-assured or fun individuality, being focused on your desires without taking away your spouse's.

The five Independent qualities show who you are as a person by having some self-focus. These are five ways to show some autonomy to pursue what you enjoy, as opposed to suppressing your drive in life. It's showing what you want in life, not over-thinking what your spouse wants all the time. The five Independent qualities are:

Be Self-Reliant

Be Personal Development Focused

Be Confident

Be Full of Life

Be Self-Fulfilling

As you go through this section, determine two things. Which quality do you find most attractive when your spouse displays it? Which quality does your spouse find most attractive when you display it? Then do the actions listed to fulfill those things for each other.

The Attraction Quiz at the end of the book can also help you and your spouse identify the quality most important to each of you.

Chapter 2

Independent Quality #1

Be Self-Reliant

Acting self-sufficient

They had fallen into a routine, but not a good routine. Chelsea was so good at, and enjoyed, organizing the household activities, Ben fell into the habit of letting her more or less run the household. She knew when they were getting low on something that needed to be picked up from the store; when the recycling truck came by; when the kids had tests and school projects that needed to be completed.

Ben fell into a pattern of just letting her take the initiative to do all of this stuff. He wasn't lazy. He helped out a lot around the house and with the kids, but he usually asked what needed to be done or how to do it. He rarely took initiative to just do something without direction.

He thought he was being a good husband by helping out whenever Chelsea needed it. What he didn't understand was that she wanted him to know when things needed to be done and to take steps to do them without asking or getting instructions from her.

For you, this is not about simply helping out around the house more. It's about knowing how to take care of things in life, especially normal daily things like the household and the kids. It's your spouse seeing that you can take care of yourself without expecting a lot of assistance in life, including inside the home.

Remember, this is about showing a kind of independence to your spouse that they would find attractive. It's being a leader along with your spouse in how the household is run. It's taking pride in how the house looks and what the kids are doing. It's showing a fire in you to be a significant part of a well-organized home.

Self-leadership of taking initiative rather than being told what to do; pride instead of complacency; and friendly competitiveness instead of laziness can all be appealing qualities to your spouse.

Show that you appreciate what they do in your domestic life together, but also that you aren't solely reliant on them for it. They want to see that you enjoy having them around, but your life isn't in shambles when they aren't around and that you can still manage normal routines with or without them being there.

Part of what your spouse may be thinking with this is if they get sick or injured that the household will carry on. They need to feel that the bills will still get paid, the family will have clean clothes, the kids will do their homework, etc. If you are doing things today that they see as irresponsible, they question whether you can do it when it needs to be done. They need to see that you can do these things now.

Know what needs to be done and, as importantly, how to do it. Then do it without needing direction or asking how, especially if it's a mess that you made. This includes normal daily household chores; paying attention to what the finances and monthly payments look like; making a note of when the kids' doctor appointments are; cooking family meals, etc.

In particular, pay close attention to the parenting of the kids. Take an active role making sure the kids go to bed on time and doing what they should be doing. Know what school projects are coming up and what after-school activities the kids are involved in. Spend some one-on-one time with each child.

Chelsea likes it when Ben is organized rather than procrastinating or putting things off until later. When he sees something is needed doing, he steps in to do it without waiting. To her, this is a sign of maturity and shows his skill to deal with things as they come up. She finds this quality of instinctively dealing with things and showing his individualistic nature very appealing.

If you don't know how to do certain things in everyday life, you can learn how to do them. There are multiple ways to learn how to do something and to practice doing it until you get good at it. Making sure you are adept at every day, domestic things can be beneficial.

Being self-reliant does not mean you each have to be financially self-reliant with your own separate income. Living off of one spouse's income is fine as long as you're both happy with that situation. You can definitely show self-reliance even if you're not the income-earner in the household.

One way is being in control of your spending and saving. Being financially responsible is a big part of being in control of your life. Find the balance between having some fun with your money today while also looking toward the future with it. Do research on personal finances to understand all aspects of it.

You have to be in control of life rather than letting life control you. This means leading your life and being responsible about not letting destructive things like drugs or alcohol overuse get the better of you or affect what you do in life.

Adept at Different Situations

Betsy hadn't thought about it. She was used to Jerry getting things ready when they went somewhere. He was good and efficient about what was needed. However, he sometimes felt she got to enjoy the activity without doing much work to get ready for it. He didn't mind doing the majority of the arranging, but he wanted to know she had some investment in it as well.

Your spouse may find it attractive when you know what to do with events and activities that are not part of the normal daily routine. Even if your spouse suggests something to do together, you can still help prepare for it. If you don't, they can perceive you as being willing to just sit back and assume they will think about everything that needs to be done.

Have a plan or be a part of making the plan. They may want you to take an active role with activities. If you do something, do it well and put full energy into it. Do it the way your spouse would see it as being self-reliant. Relying on your spouse to always do these things puts them in a "parenting" role with you in their mind, which may be a turn off to them.

Know what to do with different situations in life. Take pride in being able to figure things out. For instance, being able to read directions on how to put something together can be appealing. Another example, when going on vacation somewhere, know how to get there, what to do when you're there and how to get around once there.

This also means putting effort into other things that are more rare events and being able to figure out how to do them well. They may like it when you volunteer at the kids school or their sports/extra-curricular activities, or when you put together a special holiday dinner.

Betsy now thinks about what preparations will be needed when they go hiking together. She helps get the water bottles and snacks ready and knows the way to get there and the hiking route to take. She also researches restaurants to eat at after the hike.

Knowing what to do in all situations doesn't always come easy to everyone though, especially if your spouse automatically does things and has an order to things. There are many ways to learn how to do, or fix, something. If you can't figure how to do it, take the time to learn it.

For example, have you ever noticed your spouse rushing around doing a million things in the house before guests come over or leaving to go somewhere? Pay attention to what specific tasks they're doing. This will give you clues to what needs to be done in the future, without asking them what should be done.

Jerry and Betsy acknowledge that being handy, adept or skillful at things can be attractive as well, both with semi-common tasks outside of the home and things involving the household. Jerry finds it attractive that Betsy is very adept at parallel parking a car, while Betsy finds it attractive that Jerry is good at repairing something in the house.

However, be careful not going over-board with decisions. It can be easy to get going so fast in life that you jump to make some bigger, more important decisions by yourself. Make sure to talk over big decisions with your spouse. Remember that you can't make all sole decisions like you did when you were single.

Your Mood is Not Dependent on Their Mood

"I can't believe the size of our grocery bill! How much we spend on groceries is ridiculous." Grant was not expecting this reaction from Tina. He had come home from grocery shopping and was trying to enjoy the day with her. But now she seemed irritated about how much money was spent grocery shopping.

She does not find Grant's usual response when she does things like this to be very attractive. He would often negatively react back at her for thinking about the grocery bill instead of being in a good mood. He would be irritated, hurt, offer excuses for the bill being so high or try to defend himself in some way.

Instead, what Tina wanted from him was to not react to her mood in that manner. Sometimes it's better for him not to respond at all because she didn't really mean it in the harsh way the words came out, and her irritation is usually just in the heat of the moment and temporary. Or she wants him to make a joke to get them laughing and change the mood at that moment.

Being emotionally self-reliant is as important as being physically self-reliant. When your spouse's mood is not what you're expecting, or when their response to your mood is not what you're hoping for, the worst thing you can do is to get defensive, upset, irritated or act hurt over it.

Don't let your spouse's, or other people's, words or emotions have control over you, dictate what you do or affect you emotionally. Don't fall apart just because someone acts in a way you don't like. Let their harsher words and emotions pass without it affecting you negatively and while still staying in your own good mood. But don't ignore any real concerns they have or if you feel danger is involved.

Sometimes your spouse may say something based on the emotion they're feeling right at that moment. They may not really mean what they say in the complete context of how they said it. At times, your best response is a minimal or no response because it just ends up in an argument. This is a key point to remember – not every statement they make needs a response from you, either in person or electronically.

Sometimes you just have to let what they say go without much reaction from you. They want to see that your attitude is not reliant on what they say or do. If your emotional state stays steady, eventually the storm will pass and the sun will prevail.

They don't want you to walk on eggshells around them, or be afraid of their moods. Control your own emotions so you don't respond with defensiveness, frustration or anger. Don't try to decipher their body language or attitude to tell what kind of mood they're in.

Not only is it unhealthy for you, it can be unattractive to your spouse when you let your behavior be dependent on their behavior. You have to be emotionally strong to let them feel the way they want without being afraid of it. They want to know that you have autonomy apart from them. When you don't show this autonomy, it can come across as weak-minded on your part.

While you have compassion for them and their well-being, your happiness does not solely depend on their happiness or them acting the way you want them to. They want to know that you won't put your life on hold while waiting around for them to change dispositions or have kinder words.

Just as bad is when you try to mirror their mood or fix their frustration. Sometimes they want people around them to act normal so they can get in a better frame of mind without having other people focus on it. You don't need to try to fix or solve your spouse's mood or problem for them.

This is vital. When they are emotionally unsettled, they may not want you to be emotionally unsettled too and mirror them. Have empathy for them and don't ignore their concerns, but they may want you to be a guide for them back to a more positive mood without trying to fix the world for them.

A good way to do this and to alleviate negativity is to use humor when they seem stressed, frustrated or have unsettling words. When you feel on the verge of snapping at them because of the mood they're in or they just seem off about something, do the opposite of snapping at them.

Do something to lighten the mood or the tension they're feeling. Sometimes you just have to hold their hand and assure them it will be alright and they can trust you. Or if you can get one or both of you laughing, it may help the situation. Sometimes they're just looking to you to change the aura between you two by being fun or playful.

But if you are trying to lighten things up, don't ignore actual concerns and actions they want taken. If it's obvious this is not what they are looking for, listen to what they're asking of you. When they do express a concern out loud, they could be seeking action or a resolution, not just expressing their emotions.

When this happens, another thing to be careful about is justifying your own wrong behavior by accusing your spouse of wrong doing also, trying to deflect their legitimate concern. Even if you're correct in their short-coming, trying to bring it up now only makes you look defensive and doesn't help the marriage.

Don't Let Their Silence Affect You

Jennifer could tell something was bothering Marcus. He was quiet. Too quiet. She knew he had just completed a big assignment at work. Her first instinct was to pepper him with questions about it to see if that was why he was quiet. Maybe the assignment didn't turn out well. Maybe his boss was not pleased.

But then she remembered what he had told her last month. Let him process his feelings and emotions in his head first for a while. Sometimes Marcus needed to think about what could be done about a situation, but it was easier for him to do that inside his head than with words. Then when he was ready, he would talk about it with her.

At times, your spouse may have a need to process their stress, worries, problems and frustrations silently in their head instead of verbally out loud. Something important to them could be for them to think about their feelings and emotions without worrying what your reaction will be and no comments from you. They may not even know exactly what they're feeling yet, so trying to talk to them about it can be frustrating and unproductive.

Don't try to fix their mood if they're quiet, even if they seem upset. Sometimes they just want to be that way for a while before talking about it. Don't try to rush or disturb this process. Letting them vent silently to themselves can be what they need at times, without letting their emotions affect your emotional state.

One of the hardest things about being emotionally self-reliant is letting your spouse process their emotions and feelings in a way that's different than how you would do it. Even if it makes you uncomfortable. It may not always be easy to bite your tongue when they do this, but let them take time to themselves to think before coming to you with any kind of answers.

They are not avoiding their emotions or stuffing down their feelings. They are simply processing it in their head and dealing with their feelings differently, which may involve doing something active or physical to help alleviate their anxiety. They are not wrong in how they deal with stress, feelings or emotions, just maybe different from how you may do it. They have a right to deal with things in the way that is best for them.

The process for them may be working it out in their head first, then when they are ready to talk, they are talking about the actionable resolution they want done. They might not be seeking to talk about it in order to process what action they want or what they're feeling. Thinking to themselves in this manner can be just as productive as venting out loud to someone sometimes.

If you know something is really bothering them and you're worried about it, don't try to force them to talk because they may only go deeper into silence if they feel pressured. Instead, make them feel comfortable and able to open up to you. Think about what could be stopping them from opening up.

Their silence could be a reaction to how you yourself deal with life's frustrations. If you are overly emotional with life's stresses, your spouse may feel that they can't open up their own emotions because of what your reaction might be. They want to see emotion from you, but be careful about being over the top about it. They need to feel safe opening up their own emotions to you, but they can't feel safe if they feel you will fall apart on them when they do it.

Jennifer tends to talk a lot when something bad happens in life. She wants to communicate her feelings face to face with Marcus, which makes her feel better and is a way to cope with the stress or sorrow she's feeling. She doesn't always understand why her spouse does not do the same when he's feeling stressed.

Jennifer has to stay emotionally self-reliant to let Marcus talk out his feelings differently without letting it affect her. He typically stays quiet, but will open up about what he's feeling if he's given the right environment to do it. She is realizing that there are ways for her to help him do this, rather than thinking he should do it in the way she would.

For people who prefer to be silent about their problems, there will still be times when they will want to talk about their emotions and feelings. It will have to be in a way they're comfortable talking about them and how they want to express them, not the way their spouse would express them.

When your spouse is stressed, you can help in ways other than talking face to face and getting them to analyze how they're feeling. What they may want is your physical actions, which can be the real difference maker for their feelings. Don't focus so much on how they're feeling inside, but rather on activities you can do for them to help them to de-stress.

Sometimes they communicate better while doing something active rather than face to face. It can be talking while going for a walk; talking while cooking dinner; talking while watching a sports game. This may seem counter-intuitive to some people. How can someone concentrate on a good conversation while doing something else at the same time? For them however, it allows them to open up and sometimes talk easier if they don't have to do it while looking someone in the eye every time.

One of the ways they may deal with stress and make themselves feel better could be by doing some kind of action. They do a hobby, physical activity or something similar. They might do it by watching action such as an action movie, sports game or video game. This is a way they unwind and de-stress. While you can feel a little neglected sometimes during this time, this is an important way for them to manage stress.

Another way for them to deal with stress is to just feel neutral. They aren't really focused on thinking about or feeling anything. It doesn't mean anything bad. Sometimes it feels good to just feel nothing and let stress escape the body.

Action Plan for "Be Self-Reliant" quality

Don't need excessive assistance in life and don't get thrown off course emotionally.

Acting self-sufficient:

⊙ Know how to take care of things, including household, kids.

⊙ Be in control of your alcohol, drugs and finances.

Adept at different situations:

⊙ Know what to do and have a plan for activities, events.

⊙ Figure out how to get things done in various situations.

Your mood is not dependent on their mood:

⊙ Don't let their words or emotions affect you negatively.

⊙ Don't assess, mirror or try to fix their mood.

Don't let their silence affect you:

⊙ Let them process things silently in their head.

⊙ Don't force them to analyze feelings the way you do.

Chapter 3

Independent Quality #2

Be Personal Development Focused

Have Drive and Passion for Something

Ryan wasn't quite sure how it happened. He used to have various interests, see friends regularly, have cool experiences that he could talk about for hours and be driven towards something in life. All of this stopped somewhere during life, marriage and having a family.

The most intriguing thing was not how it affected him, but how it affected Stephanie. She didn't really see it while it was happening, but when he gradually stopped all of this, she realized how attractive that him using his mind and having his own passions is to her. She missed him doing these things and having him talk about it.

She likes a balance in life when he doesn't do this and just turns his mind off to enjoy fun, carefree times. But what she really finds attractive is when he actively engages his mind to show drive and passion about something in life and to pursue some form of self-development or mental stimulation.

Being passionate about something and showing determination can be very appealing to your spouse. Having activities outside of the marriage, your spouse, and your family is part of what demonstrates drive and motivation as a person. It adds creativity and variety to your life and shows you have focus.

You're showing your spouse that you're an interesting, impressive person outside of being just a parent or partner. They want to see you're focusing on your own happiness, challenging yourself, exploring life and have something of quality going on with your life overall.

It's the joyfulness you show for something, the knowledge you have about it and your ability to have a conversation around it that can be appealing. They like to see you have aspiration in life, both at work and outside of it, and have relevant stories or things to talk about.

Stephanie told Ryan that his doing these things in moderation doesn't take away from their relationship. It actually increases his attractiveness, despite him focusing on himself. Him taking some time to focus on himself actually makes her happy, as long as it's a reasonable amount of time.

Occasionally focusing on yourself can show people who you are as an individual. Just like when taking a picture, the background and what you're doing in it are as important as your face because it gives people a better sense of who you are as an overall person and your interests. Here are some ways to do this.

Have an interest or hobby. It doesn't matter what your interest or hobby is. It's just the feeling you give your spouse of being involved with something instead of just sitting around doing nothing. Hobbies and interests give you something interesting to talk about, both to your spouse and to others.

If you don't already have a hobby or interest, try different things until you find one that you have a passion for. It can give you something to look forward to and can help you be a happier person overall.

Interests don't have to be something active you do, they can just be something you read about, watch or listen to.

In addition, find one or two little things to look forward to each week. This can help you keep an upbeat attitude because you have something to anticipate during the week, even if it's small, and help get you through the mundane parts of life easier.

See/talk to friends. Seeing or chatting with friends, and catching up on their lives, gives you something to look forward to. This helps you be interesting because you can talk to your spouse about what's going on in your friends' lives and exposes you to different things through their eyes.

Something that's important, but difficult, is to assess how your current friends affect your life and your happiness. Do you feel better or worse after talking with a particular friend? Do you feel motivated to improve your life or do they drag you down a little bit? Make sure your current friendships are adding to your happiness and development, not taking away from it.

Have experiences or adventures. Doing something different helps to make you a well-rounded person and can allow you to tell compelling stories and experiences. Travel is one way to do this, but an experience can be as simple as going with a friend to a restaurant you normally wouldn't go to. Just simply try new things to give you something to talk about later. Even if you don't enjoy a new activity, it's good to open up your horizons.

Increase knowledge, mental stimulation. Increasing knowledge is a little about increasing intelligence, but also more than that. It allows you add to conversations with knowledgeable facts or open to ideas. It allows you to clearly communicate the things you've learned and know something about.

One way to increase knowledge is to listen to different types of things as background noise. Instead of always listening to your favorite music station, put on a news station, a motivational advice station, etc. If you're busy in the kitchen, put on a TV station or other entertainment source. It's amazing how much you can absorb when you listen to things.

It's about self-development and knowing something you didn't know yesterday. It's about opening up your mind to things you hadn't thought of before. Read different kinds of books and listen to different types of things than you usually would. Having an open mind instead of a closed mind is important and attractive.

Don't just use knowledge to show a better way to do something. You don't want to hide your intelligence, but showing off might be perceived as a way of being judgmental and looking down on people. Use your knowledge as a way to be interesting and enjoy a two-sided conversation.

Be good at something. Learning or continuing to develop a skill or activity shows you're good at it, but it also shows perseverance on your part to improve at that skill or activity. Your spouse may want to watch you do something you're good at, both at work and outside of it. Have determination to take the time and effort to practice and become good at it, rather than just giving up because it's hard.

This is where continually learning, studying, practicing and repetition is important, because it's difficult to be good at something if you don't do these things. Showing the determination it takes to be impressive at a skill or activity can be very appealing to your spouse.

Dreams and aspirations. Have dreams and aspirations, in your job and in life in general. Think about what you want out of life now and in the future. It can be having a purpose or path in life you want to go, or it can simply be something fun and adventurous you want to do.

No matter what you do for work, be proud of it. Talk about it like it's the greatest job in the world. If it's a stepping stone to another job, talk about your next career move but don't downplay your current job. You can also find unique things about the industry itself to talk about. It's attractive when you are proud of your job no matter what anyone else thinks of it.

At the same time, don't over-stress if your career isn't where you want it to be. If you get overly frustrated or down about it, that can actually work against you. Just keep thinking positive and moving forward. When opportunities arise, take advantage of them, but don't put too much pressure on yourself to know exactly where you should be going in life all the time.

Condensing it down. What a lot of this comes down to is simply being interesting to your spouse and to others. You can talk about your hobbies, interests and friends with a passion. Your spouse can watch you do a skill or activity that you're good at. They can hear your stories about experiences you've had or your knowledge of different subjects. They can see the determination you have at work, and with life itself.

Dedication to Health, Hygiene, Appearance

"Have I been walking around all day with this stain on my shirt?" he wondered. Gavin got comfortable in life. He got a little stagnant. He used to make sure his shirts were clean and not wrinkled when he went to work. He used to dress a little better when going out to dinner. He used to eat better, exercise and notice if his weight was affecting his health. Gavin hadn't done any of these things in a long time. Too long.

Dedication, and being motivated to fully commit to it, may be appealing to your spouse. In this case, the motivation and dedication to live an active, healthy lifestyle. Do things for good grooming, attentive hygiene and maintaining healthy habits. Being conscious of your well-being and taking pride in your visual presence is a factor, as well as showing a consistent effort.

This aspect is a component of the overall concept of being persistent and not being complacent. They may want to see you developing in different areas of your life and this is just one of them. Challenge yourself to be your best physical version while also being happy with yourself, having a positive body image and a good mindset around it. Balance self-development with being proud of how you are now.

The health part includes watching what you eat, exercising regularly and developing some muscle. The behavior that may appeal to them is the discipline that it takes to consistently do these things. But be aware that judging or saying rude hurtful things about people, even yourself, is never okay.

Exercising has many benefits outside of just how you look physically. It can be good for your lungs and your heart. It can be good for elevating your mood and helping depression. It can be good for you physically, emotionally and psychologically. This is part of showing your spouse that you care about having a robust mind as well as body.

Watch your nutrition, eat well, don't smoke and don't drink excessively. Your spouse wants both of you to help take care of each other in later years of life, and they don't want you to have health problems because of poor habits. Pay attention to things like how much sodium, sugar and fattening foods you consume.

Hygiene is an extension of health and putting in effort. When you show good hygiene habits, it shows you are thinking about your health overall. This can include different aspects such as dental hygiene, your breath, body odor, foot odor, trimming various body hair, nail trimming and smelling good with certain types of soap or fragrances.

General cleanliness and personal body grooming are an important aspect of hygiene, including making sure your hair is clean and maintained. Having a good haircut and hairstyle can make a difference too. Good posture isn't part of hygiene but is part of taking pride in yourself visually.

Your clothing is an aspect of showing you care about how you present yourself visually. If you look sloppy with wrinkled or ill-fitting clothes, you can look like you don't care about your appearance or health, even if you are healthy. Make sure the clothes are not wrinkled, dirty or stained when you wear them.

Think about how your clothes fit and if they are at least a little stylish and somewhat modern. You don't need to spend a lot of money on expensive clothes. Just make sure your clothes aren't too loose, too tight or very faded and old looking. Put a little attention to fashion trends, what other people are wearing and small aspects of your wardrobe.

Wear different types of outfits that suit both your mood and the outing. Dress well, but dress for the occasion without overdoing it or looking out of place. Wear nicer clothes going out somewhere than you would simply running errands. Wear casual or sporty clothes when you're doing something active. Wear different shoes at dinner than you would going for a walk.

Too much focus on the visual aspect of yourself can have the opposite effect of what you're wanting to achieve though. It can make you look like you're trying too hard, not being real or seeking too much attention. You need to find the right balance between putting in effort of being attentive with your clothing but not overdoing it.

Have Ambition and Goals

Kate took life as it came at her. This was a good quality because she lived in the moment. But Tom was attracted to her in the times when she would set a goal for herself and see her tenacity to make that achievement. Too often, because she was an in-the-moment person, she wouldn't also have an eye toward the future.

Use personal development to push yourself with goals and ambition in life. Look at the commitment, persistence and relentlessness you have toward achieving what you want in life. The first staple with goals and ambition is having a solid work ethic. No matter what you're doing, at your job or away, give 100% effort and do it the best you can.

Set a goal for yourself and work toward improving it. One of the most beneficial things to do is to think about what you want in all areas and timelines of your life, then make a plan on how to achieve them. If you want to be better at an activity, you may have to research on how to be better at it and devote time to doing it.

Time and effort. There is simply no substitute for achieving goals other than investing lots of time in it and putting in maximum effort toward it. For instance, at work you can put in some extra hours to develop your skills. You can mentor with someone senior to you, either inside the company or outside of it. You can take on-line classes to learn something different or to enhance what you already do.

To achieve what you want in life may mean you have to work harder than others do. Don't whine, complain or boast about it. Just choose to do it and be content with it. You can't assume success, you have to work hard at it and earn it. It's action-oriented by continually taking little steps to achieve your goals.

Not letting things stand in your way of whatever success or goal you want can be highly attractive. There's a fine line between understanding that achieving most goals is a lot of hard work, but not letting that stop you in the first place. Find the motivation to start a goal and the motivation to keep going even when it's difficult. This is where taking the little steps helps.

Kate found that just making small goals is what made the difference for her larger goal. She was upset that she hadn't started saving for retirement yet, but her income is tight. So she started with a small goal of saving just 2% of her paycheck. Then she will increase it by 1% every few months.

One factor of ambition is making sure the environment around you is motivating to you, not de-motivating. Figure out how you re-charge your energy – being around people more or being alone more. Figure out the things that help you stay positive – shows to watch; music to listen to; friends to be around. Figure out what makes you feel optimistic – work; hobbies; being active; religion/spiritual things; motivational books or speeches.

You become more interesting and have things to talk about when you are ambitious because you allow yourself to explore, experiment and try new things. Do this both in your personal life and at whatever work you do, whether that's a job, staying home or doing volunteer work.

You may also find that other people are going through what you're going through, which means you may be able to help each other. But you would never know that if you don't talk to people about it and let them know what you're exploring, trying to experiment with and have ambition toward.

It's good to have internal fortitude to achieve goals in life, but don't let it over-stress you. Having ambition doesn't mean you have everything figured out. A lot of times you won't have things figured out in life and that's okay too. Putting too much pressure on yourself can have a detrimental effect on your mental well-being or steer you into doing the wrong thing.

Having goals doesn't mean you know exactly what your future will look like. It just simply means that you will move forward and continue to think about where you want to go in life without feeling pressure to know today what that exact path is.

Overcome Obstacles, Even Own Flaws

Christy had a habit of talking about problems like they were mountains. Not mountains to overcome and conquer, but mountains that couldn't be traversed. Fear would make her hesitant. She had to find a way to realize that she was bigger than the issues in her life, not the other way around.

Focusing on personal development doesn't mean you are perfect the way you are. You know you have your own flaws and that problems happen in life. Look at how you're striving to improve weaknesses, and at how you respond after you get knocked down in life.

Realize that admitting your faults is not the problem. The problem is ignoring your faults and not striving to overcome them. Be honest about your mistakes and flaws, but show the desire to be better. You want forgiveness for any transgressions, but you ultimately want to improve for yourself. You are striving to do what's right, not what's easy.

Having problems or a difficult past is not something to be ashamed of. Making mistakes in life is not a negative thing. It's how you deal with those mistakes afterwards is what really counts. Everyone has their own issues and problems. It gives your spouse the opportunity to see that they can be an influence in your life, but that you yourself are the driving force to get past them.

Obstacles and difficult situations will arise in life, but have a plan on how to deal with them and move past them. You can show emotions, but let your spouse know you are in control of the situation, rather than the situation being in control of you. Their fear is not that you show emotions, it's that you will fall apart and allow other things to be in control of your life.

Use setbacks as fuel to get better and view them as a personal challenge. If you get knocked down, find a motivation to get back up and come back with twice the strength. Even with hardships in life, it's up to you to choose the right path and to turn a negative into a positive.

Learning how to effectively cope with disappointment is invaluable. Realize that you will have periodic disappointing times and everyone goes through it. Life is full of ups and downs. The down moments can be very frustrating, but the key is to recognize the down times won't last forever and to truly appreciate the up moments in life.

When you talk about a problem, make sure you don't act like the problem is bigger than you can handle. Make sure you express that while it may be a problem now, you will figure out a way to defeat it instead of it defeating you. They know that everyone has problems/issues to deal with in life, but they want to know that you won't crumble when dealing with them.

Building mental strength and focus takes perseverance. Dealing with life's difficulties, but not letting them hold you down for long, is what builds mental strength and helps you face the next challenge. It also means avoiding making excuses, feeling sorry for yourself or blaming others for not achieving your goals.

Think through it before committing to do something. Don't say you're going to do something if you have no good way of doing it. If you say you'll do it anyway, don't bury your head in the sand and forget about it. Figure out a way to get it done in a timely manner and similar to how you said you'd do it.

Ask for advice, guidance or help if you need it and be willing to accept it. Asking for help is not a bad thing at all, but ignoring it could be problematic. Your spouse wants to see you deal with problems in a healthy way. Use them as a learning experience and find a way to deal with them effectively.

Sometimes this is easier said than done, so don't be afraid to talk to a therapist or counselor. It's easy to think that what you are going through is incredibly bad and no one else can relate to it, but just realize that you're not alone. Talking to someone about it can be incredibly valuable for your mental health.

Action Plan for "Be Personal Development Focused" quality

Be interesting through your own personal development and determination in life.

Have drive and passion for something:

- ⊙ Have passion for interests, hobbies, friends.
- ⊙ Expand knowledge and be good at something.

Dedication to health, hygiene, appearance:

- ⊙ Assess your nutrition, hygiene, grooming, clothes.
- ⊙ Exercise for mental, emotional and physical health.

Have ambition and goals:

- ⊙ Strive toward goals in life and challenge yourself.
- ⊙ Don't assume success; work hard and earn it.

Overcome obstacles, even own flaws:

- ⊙ Be honest about mistakes, but work to overcome them.
- ⊙ Use setbacks in life as fuel to be bigger than problems.

Chapter 4

Independent Quality #3

Be Confident

Assertive

Mason had always been a passive person. He didn't want to sound bossy, demanding or pushy. He prided himself on being congenial and making sure everyone was happy.

Melissa had to clarify that she liked this trait of his, but she also found it attractive when he stated what his own desires were in a straight-forward manner. She knew he always looked out for her happiness, so she wasn't the least bit offended when he made a bold statement about what he wanted.

Don't let fear, guilt or embarrassment stop you from pursuing your desires or actions you want to take. Don't be afraid to focus on what you want in life and what will make you happy. Your spouse knows there's a difference between this and being selfish by only doing things you want without regard for them.

They want you to be bold and assertive when you want to do something instead of being timid or passive about it. Straight forward honesty and an assured tone of voice about what you want and like can be what your spouse is looking for. You project confidence when you are respectfully assertive in this way.

Confidence can come across with how you say something as much as what you say. Form things as a statement when you want something because forming it as a question can sometimes come across as passive or hesitant. Tell them what you want and like, or do the action of what you want instead of tentatively asking for it. It can be attractive when you know what you want and aren't afraid to do it or to plainly state it in a polite way.

Also make sure they understand it's not something you're kind of wishing for. You can say "let's do x" instead of "I want to do x", which can sound like a future wish not a current desire. They are usually okay with this because they trust that you will listen to them if they do have a different preference.

In addition, it can take the burden off of them wondering if you actually want something. It's a balance between stating what you want, but not making a demand like you're their boss. Melissa likes Mason to say, "Let's go to the Italian restaurant tonight," instead of "Do you want to go out to dinner tonight?" However, he's ready to change plans if she has a different idea. He doesn't get stuck into being rigid about it.

But at the same time, don't automatically give in every time your desires conflict or they want something else. If you give in to what they want the majority of the time, that's not fair to you. Someone may temporarily be denied getting what they want, but that doesn't have to be you the majority of the time.

It sounds odd, but acquiescing to their desires all the time is not attractive to them because they know it's not right and not equal, even if they don't outwardly show it at the time. Both spouses should take turns sacrificing for each other. It's partially about being comfortable saying "no" to them at times, but it's mainly about simply sticking to what you desire some of the time.

Suggest doing new things together that you want to try. Often there may be times when you will want to do something new and they will get as much enjoyment out of it as you do. This is a great way to show them something, while also trying out new things you're interested in doing.

Even if your spouse doesn't want to do something you want to do, don't be afraid to do it yourself, as long as it doesn't go against their values. Being assertive and having determination about what you want to do without letting someone stop you can be attractive to them.

This shows that you will pursue what you want in life without letting other people deter you. You won't give up easily for what you truly want out of life. You're showing you will mold your life in the way you want and fulfilling to you.

Being assertive doesn't mean they will automatically do and say whatever you want. Your spouse wants you to be honest about what you want and do what makes you happy, but they also want the ability to decide if they want to fulfill this for you. There's a big difference between simply stating what you want and expecting them to comply every time.

There will be times where you will be assertive about what you want and run into resistance from your spouse. You have to find a balance of respecting their response while also remaining self-assured. Here are some suggestions for this balance.

Take their "no" seriously by dropping it and letting it go at that moment, unless it's a big decision you feel strongly about. The more you try to talk them into it, the more frustrated they will feel and resistant to it because they feel their response isn't being taken seriously. Don't act hurt over it or let it change your mood.

This really helps if they want to do it, but it's just bad timing. If they are in the middle of doing something else, they may automatically say no while thinking in the back of their head that they would be happy to do it later on after they're done. By not guilting them about it or letting it alter your disposition toward them, they may be excited to meet your request later.

If they give you a hesitation but not a no, use some lightness or banter/playful words to see if it really is an absolute no. But do it without coercing them, sounding whiny or like you're begging. You're verifying since they didn't give you a definitive answer. But most important, show them you will stay in a good mood regardless of what their answer is.

Take one thing at a time. If you are wanting them to do multiple things at once, it could be over-whelming to them. They may have said yes to one thing, but when over-whelmed they will say no to everything. Let them get comfortable with one thing they are hesitant about before moving on to something else.

Finally, slow and patient can be your two best friends. If your idea seems big to them, break it down into little steps to do slowly over time so it doesn't seem so big. Let them get comfortable one small step at a time because you are probably 20 steps ahead of them in thinking about, and accepting, this new thing.

Direct and to the Point

Brittany was fuming. She didn't understand why Drew didn't get it. She thought she was clear about what she wanted to do that day with him. She told him last week that she was looking forward to the weather changing and going on a hike together. Then this morning she mentioned how sunny it was outside. Instead, they were sitting inside a movie theater.

After the movie, they talked about this miscommunication. Drew said that the movie was going to be leaving the theaters soon and he wanted to see it before it left, but he would have suggested they see it after the hike if she had clearly stated she wanted to go on a hike that morning while it was sunny.

Brittany realized he was right. He never ignored her when she specifically stated that she wanted to do something. They could have easily accommodated both of their desires that day if she had been direct and to the point about what she wanted.

Be direct and to the point of what's on your mind. Expecting your spouse to comprehend hints, read your mind or instinctively know what you want is a set up for disappointment and arguments. You might think it's obvious what you want, but it's often not obvious to them.

It's crucial to take the time to let them know explicitly what you're thinking and how you're feeling so there's no miscommunication. You can't expect them to put importance on something when you don't tell them it is important to you. Asking if they would like to do something is not the same thing as saying, "this is important to me, please do it."

Some people like structure and having a plan set forth in front of them. You being direct and to the point may give your spouse this structure they like feeling. If they stay within certain guidelines that they're comfortable with, they can feel safe both emotionally and physically.

Not with everything, but sometimes they want you to take charge and lead a situation. They may want to follow your cues and can feel frustrated when you won't take this lead at times. They may even be okay with you sounding somewhat stern, but without being overbearing. Say what's on your mind, but without being rude or insensitive. Remember though that things still must be agreed on together.

Saying what's on your mind also includes being direct about things they do or say that bugs you. Definitely don't do this with everything and sound nit-picky, but let them know when they repeatedly do things that could turn into a major issue for you. This is for things that could wear on you over the long term, but do it in a calm fashion, not hostile, snide or sarcastic.

No one is perfect, so sometimes they need a little reminder that they're over-reacting to something. Like everyone, they aren't always conscious of how they sound to others or when they're being unreasonable. So they don't want you to pretend that this behavior is okay. If something upsets you, tell them, but do it in a respectful way.

They might initially be taken back by this and be a little upset at first. But that short term upset is better than long term problems. Always look to the long term. Will what you're about to push back on help the relationship in the future? This is what they find appealing –

the fact that you're thinking about the long term health of the relationship, not avoiding short term upset feelings.

It also shows that you are taking responsibility for your own actions or lack of action. If you choose not to say something that bothers you, you can't blame them later on. If you choose to do something that you regret later, you can't say it's their fault. If you aren't direct with them, you can't be upset at them if you realize either of you made a bad decision.

They may want you to change from a vague, general statement into a request that motivates them to take action. Instead of Brittany saying, "This kitchen is a mess," she now says "I need help because I'm running late today. Would you mind cleaning up the kitchen while I do the laundry." She also uses a pleasant tone when saying it, which is vital.

"I feel" statements can be good to use when you want to convey an emotion to your spouse, but be careful using them if you have a specific action you want taken by them. For action, a better way is for you to phrase it in terms of "I need", "I want" or "I would like" when you truly know what you want from them.

When you start sentences with those phrases, their instinct to make you happy kicks in. They think, "I know exactly what they want and can help them." Your spouse knows what action to take to help you because you're being specific.

Another way to be more specific to your spouse is to turn your request into a question by replacing "I want" with "what is." If it makes sense as a question, then the request is too vague and should be more specific. An example would be, "I want more affection." The question would be, "What is more affection?" Since you can turn your request into a legitimate question, it shows your request is too vague and needs to be more specific.

However, if you say "I want you to give me a hug in the morning", it would turn into "What is give me a hug in the morning?" That question does not make sense and therefore the request is specific enough for them to take action on.

Also be careful with vague requests that could be fulfilled in different ways. "I want more romance" is a vague statement. Your idea of more romance might be candlelight dinners and walks holding hands. But their idea might be making you popcorn to eat while watching TV together or giving you flowers. If you have specific ideas about how you would like a request filled, then you have to tell them specifically what it is.

When you ask your spouse for something, be both direct and polite. Saying "I had a really tiring day at work" is being polite, but not direct that you want help making dinner. Saying "get off the couch and help with dinner" is direct, but not polite.

Saying "I could use some help. Can you cut the vegetables while I make the sauce" is both direct and polite. Or if they pick a restaurant you don't like, be nice in stating you would prefer a different one.

Be careful how you go about this, but being direct also includes being honest about something they do that turns you off. Not minor things, but things that truly affect your respect or romantic view of them. Don't be insensitive, but be honest so you don't start viewing them in a light that will hurt your connection.

It's easy to be insensitive when you are direct and to the point. Being direct does not mean you can say whatever is on your mind at any time. You still have to be careful what you say and take their feelings into consideration. You have a right to be heard, but don't become overbearing and intense. Take all blame and accusatory tone out of the communication. Don't try to get what you want by degrading someone else.

Decisive

"What should we do for dinner tonight?" She knew what his response to her question was going to be before it even came out of his mouth, and it made her cringe just thinking about it.

Because Kyle was trying to be amenable to Lindsey, it became his default response to just let her pick, even when she asked for his opinion. This grew to be an irritation to her after a while because it felt like a burden to her now. She had to think ahead of time what to do or where to go because he never would.

Your spouse likes it when you have an opinion about something they ask about, and they like it when you make a decision when given an option between things. To do this, eliminate or cut down on phrases such as "I don't care" or "Whatever you want". When you make a decision, don't waver on it. Stick to your decisions unless given a valid reason why you should re-consider.

While you think you may be cordial letting them pick what to do or where to go, to them it may just come across as you being unable to make a decision or too lazy to make a decision. Being amenable is good in a relationship, but doing it too much can look lazy, indecisive and weak to them. It's okay to take charge on occasion, as long as you don't do it all the time or act controlling.

Don't expect them to make all the decisions. If the car needs an oil change, take care of it. If something is not working properly, look into having it fixed. If a bill needs to be paid, pay it. Don't take away all decisions from them and don't act like they're incapable of doing something. Just don't act like you're expecting them to do it all.

There is a fine line between asking your spouse's opinion on matters that involve both of you, and asking their opinion on everything. They definitely want to be included in big decisions, but sometimes they want you to just make a decision on smaller things without asking their opinion.

It may sound like you're being a good partner to ask their opinion a lot, but to them it could sound like you're not confident in your own decision making ability and that you don't want to be responsible for the outcome if something goes wrong. You can be viewed as weak by them, even when you just mean to sound like you're not wanting to exclude them.

Don't be apprehensive worrying about how they will react when you do stuff or to how you do it. Even if they react badly to something, don't let it overly affect you and don't feel obligated to change it just because they say so. Change it if it makes sense or is really important to them.

Worried you'll make the wrong decision and something will go wrong? Make another decision to correct it and move on. Your spouse doesn't expect you to be perfect. They just expect you to correct a problem that's been caused by one of your decisions. The key is to make decisions that don't have life-altering effects. If you do make a decision that's life-altering, do your research first and know you're making a good choice given all the options and circumstances.

You need to direct life, don't let life direct you. Change happens in life and people look up to those who can be decisive, deal with it and move forward, rather than falling apart or getting frustrated over it. Show confidence by embracing change. Show unwavering calm in the midst of a problem.

Lindsey doesn't want Kyle to dictate, but she does want him to state his opinion and know a way of doing it. Being swayed by everyone else's opinions is not what she finds attractive. Having the confidence to state this, stick to it and not let his emotions sway him from it is what she finds appealing.

Have an opinion about things, know what you want and have a plan for getting it. This includes little plans in life as well as big plans. When you don't do these things, it's easier to get manipulated by other people, which is not what your spouse wants to see. It can also make you apologize for things you shouldn't be apologizing for.

Stand Up For Your Values

Amber is relatively short and petite, and her personality is more of a follower than a leader. Because of her physical stature and her innate persona, she often went along with things that she knew she shouldn't because they didn't line up with her values and morals. This usually wasn't with her husband, but more with her friends and family. Robert found a strong attraction to her though when she did respectfully stand up for her values and morals, both with him and outside of the marriage.

There are two main points to standing up for yourself. First, there is nothing physical about this. This is not about physically compelling someone to do something or using anger to convey your message. It's okay to show emotion, just make sure it doesn't spill over into hostile anger.

Second, it's not about demanding or coercing them to do something, or to agree with you. They are their own person and get to choose what they do. However, you are simply stating what your values and morals are and what you will do. What they're doing may be unacceptable to you, but ultimately, they get to decide if they want to continue their behavior or not.

This is about using your words, tone and attitude to get people, including your spouse, to think about how their actions are affecting you. Calmly and respectfully get them to question if they are being reasonable at that moment. You are giving them the choice to change their own actions or telling them no in a civil manner if they ask something of you that you can't do or is unreasonable.

You have a right to say what goes against your principles. And to not back down from it. Let your spouse know if they want you to do something inappropriate, bad timing, them being lazy, overly controlling or truly unacceptable to you based on your values. They respect people who stand up for themselves without yelling, demanding or trying to force obedience.

Say something when they are being dismissive of your concerns or something that's bothering you; when they aren't being careful about harsh words they're using toward you; or when they're making excuses not to do what's important to you. It's not okay for them to treat what's important to you as trivial.

Don't be afraid of conflict, but don't get into a drawn-out argument over it. Just make your statement and leave it at that. Sometimes fewer words are best. Don't get sucked into a back-and-forth discussion that is only argumentative and unproductive. You're not trying to win an argument or force them to concede your point. You're only stating your viewpoint.

Don't expect them to immediately see your side of things. They may see those things later on after cooling down, or they may never see them the way you do. The point is that you see it. Even if they don't agree or are upset with your stance, your fortitude to do this may be attractive to them.

Not showing anger is the key. People can often react negatively to your emotion rather than to what you're actually saying. Your words can be invisible to them because they can't see past your emotional response. Stay calm to let them actually hear your words and your conviction behind them.

Even though she was upset by what he said to her, Amber made a simple statement to Robert with no sign of anger. "You would not want me insulting you. So if you would like to rephrase that without an insult, I would be happy to respond."

Another example is to ask them a question. "Are you asking me to do this favor for you or are you demanding something?" Often, they may not even realize they may be coming across in such a demanding or condescending way. This is a simple, non-argumentative way of reminding them of your need for politeness.

They may get a little frustrated with you when you do this. It's human nature. We all think our way is the right way in the heat of the moment. Being frustrated doesn't mean they don't respect your ability to stand up for your values and for what you think is right, so stay firm with your standards despite their initial reaction.

Low standards can be a turn off to your spouse. If you will accept any kind of behavior from people, even your spouse, towards you, that can be very unattractive in their eyes. Alternately, if you refuse to put up with unacceptable behavior toward you, or toward people that you care about, that can be attractive to them.

You have a right to say "no" to your spouse if something goes against your morals and values. Know what your morals and values are and be steadfast about them. Don't let people make you question or compromise your ethics, even your spouse. It's important for you to both know what each other's values are, and to respect them.

Just because you want them to be happy doesn't mean you have to give up your own happiness in exchange. It doesn't mean they have to do it, but you can't let them make you feel guilty just because your desires are different than theirs. Truly believe that your needs, wants and desires are as valid as your spouse's.

Having good standards also includes holding people, including your spouse, to put their full effort into things when it directly affects you. In these cases, it's okay to hold them accountable and challenge them to meet realistic expectations, while also holding yourself to the same standards. The key is to show them that you're standing right alongside of them and won't ask them to do anything you're not doing yourself.

You can feel confident doing this when you know you have integrity. You don't put others down to make yourself look better. You don't do or say things to others you wouldn't want done or said to you. You're not a hypocrite or have double standards. You hold yourself to a high standard before expecting others to be at a high standard.

Believe in Yourself

Self-esteem can be a tricky thing. Craig often felt lucky in life. He was lucky to find and marry a wonderful wife, land a great job and have good friends. However, he felt he got these things due to luck rather than his own good traits.

Michelle married him because he was better than any man she had ever dated; he landed his job because he worked hard and put in time to know his craft as good as anyone; he has good friends because he puts in effort to maintain those relationships. Craig has a reason to have high self-esteem because of who he is, not because of luck.

Show confidence in who you are as a person. Know you're not perfect, but don't feel guilty or ashamed of the way you are. Be comfortable with yourself and self-assured, regardless of the situation. Developing good self-esteem and self-worthiness can have a positive impact on your actions and behavior.

Your spouse wants to see your belief in yourself and know your own worth. They want to see you believe you are on an equal level with everyone else, especially with them. Believe your qualities are good and you don't have to feel bad about them. Having confidence in yourself without over-worrying about any perceived short-comings is highly attractive.

It's an attitude that leads your life. Know you are worthy of something great to be part of your life. You are fortunate to be with your spouse, but also believe they are fortunate to be with you too. You are fortunate to have your job, but they are also fortunate to have you as an employee. This has to come across in your words, actions and overall attitude.

Find little motivations that spark a fire in you and focuses you on what you want, and are, in life. Something internal or external that really pushes you to believing that you can and will achieve something if you want it. Establish in your mind what you're trying to achieve, if anything, and ascend to it. Don't back down from knowing who you are and what you're aspiring for.

Use external noise as motivation, not as discouragement. There will always be people and situations questioning you, your abilities or your qualities. Sage advice is to not listen to the distractions, but that's often really difficult to do. So then it comes down to either letting it discourage you or motivate you.

To go along with this, have a strong belief in your abilities of whatever you're doing. Believe you can and will do well at what you're doing at the moment. You may find your results can actually improve if you simply think you will succeed rather than fail. The power of the mind can be amazing.

Don't let someone try to guilt you into accepting a definition of yourself that you know is not correct. If someone, even your spouse, accuses you of something that you know is not accurate, don't just roll over and accept it. It's okay for others to shine, but don't let them knock you down to do it.

Don't doubt yourself just because someone said something negative about you. You don't always have to agree with everything they say. If you truly believe they are wrong about you, it's okay to push back a little and show who you are. Don't do this with every little thing, but doing it at times when you truly believe in something can be appealing to your spouse. They don't want you to be their puppet, agreeing with everything.

Have confidence in yourself by not being afraid or ashamed of qualities about yourself. If someone tries to badmouth a quality you like about yourself, don't back down from it. Don't try to defend yourself or get into an argument over it. Just simply own up to that quality and readily admit you have that quality and are proud of it.

By the same token, if you do something different in life than other people, don't feel that you have to change to be like them. Your spouse wants to see that you have the courage to be different than other people if that's what you desire and that you won't succumb to peer pressure.

You can take advice from people, but ultimately you are responsible for your life and your decisions. It is your life and you get to choose how you want to live it and what makes you happy. Work on being mentally strong enough to project this kind of strength and confidence.

One way to help achieve this is to read or listen to inspirational or self-help things. Everybody can use a boost to their self-esteem once in a while, so this is a good way to do that, along with talking to someone if you feel that would help.

You don't have to be perfect at everything, or even above average. Just be confident in what life has to offer you, and to not settle for less, because you are worthy of it. This demeanor can be contagious. When you show confidence with life, other people look up to you, want to follow you and believe in this as well. As with anything, be careful not to take this too far. Have confidence, but don't overly pat yourself on the back.

Confident body language can help too. Your spouse may like it when you have good posture, standing up straight, no hunched shoulders. Keep your head up as you're walking and looking people in the eyes when you talk. Speak confidently, instead of acting nervous or unsure of yourself.

Have courage to do things that are uncomfortable to you. Don't let fear or anxiety stop you from doing things in life. It can be impressive to your spouse to see this type of boldness and fortitude from you toward things.

If you feel your spouse may be nervous about something, be a steady rock for them. Even if you're nervous too, do your best to hide it to help them feel at ease in uncomfortable situations. When you show no sign of nerves, it's a calming effect. Show them you have things under control and everything will be fine.

It's normal to get nervous, but when you try to put aside your nervousness and be relaxed, it helps you be yourself and lets your regular personality shine through. Acting too nervous can hide your personality and make you seem like a different person than who you are. Showing confidence to try to overcome that nervousness can be reassuring and very attractive to your spouse.

Action Plan for "Be Confident" quality

Show you're self-assured regardless of the situation you're in and bold about things in life.

Assertive:

- Say what you want with a statement, not tentatively asking.
- Don't automatically give in when your desires conflict.

Direct and to the point:

- Be direct, specific and lead sometimes.
- If something bothers you, say it calmly.

Decisive:

- Make decisions and have opinions.
- Have a plan and act on it.

Stand up for your values:

- Calmly be firm about your standards, morals and values.
- Know your abilities, qualities and worth are equal to others.

Believe in yourself:

- Be self-assured in situations, without nervousness.
- Find little motivations that will spark a fire in you.

Chapter 5

Independent Quality #4

Be Full of Life

Live in the Moment

Somewhere along the way, William developed a very structured life. Andrea likes it when he can break out of that box at times. She wants to see him put a priority and focus on excitement and enjoyment in life, both for her sake and for his own. She wants him to know what truly makes him happy and pleases him. She wants to see him be carefree and have a short "time-out" on occasion from the normal, ordinary routine.

She likes a balance in life when he doesn't do this and activates his mind or actively engages his brain when he needs to. But what she really finds attractive is when he can turn it off and just let loose to live in the moment, enjoy what life has to offer at that time and just be fun-loving.

A part of your spouse's happiness may simply come from seeing you happy, doing things that you want to do or really looking forward to, and just having fun in life. This includes both in the home and out. Keep an eye on the future, but don't forget to take a break from regular life and simply live for today too.

They want to see that spontaneous, fiery side of you coming out at times. Think of a celebration at the end of a sports game when your team wins and everyone is going crazy. It's not necessarily about being that over-the-top; it's simply about not thinking, or worrying, about tomorrow. You're not being self-conscious of your actions and you're not trying to impress anyone. You're just having fun in the moment!

Life can be serious and stressful. Sometimes they want to put all of that out of their mind for a little while and just let go. They want to let their mind go blank on the normal adult cares and responsibilities. They want to hit the pause button on anything that takes too much brain power or times that have too much seriousness to them without an element of playfulness to it.

You can give them a temporary escape from their regular life and who they are expected to be in everyday life. Having a daily routine or thought-provoking discussions are not bad things, but your timing might be off if they're looking for something different once in a while. Save these occasions for another time. Do, or say, things that will allow their mind to forget about anything stressful for a while. Focus on being light during this time.

Break up the monotony of normal life, at home and outside of it. It doesn't necessarily have to be anything elaborate, wild or crazy. It can be as simple as trying a new event you've never done. Just something different to get your senses, and your spouses' senses, activated because it's new.

Andrea wants William to initiate plans to do fun and exciting things occasionally, both with or without her. She likes doing things with him, but also wants to know he's not afraid to do those things without her being involved. He will say, "do you want to go with me to do x?" This shows he wants her to come enjoy the fun with him, but isn't afraid to do it without her.

One trap that is easy to fall into is to over-focus on your spouse's happiness or preferences during this time. What you may not realize is that outwardly showing your own joy is also important to their satisfaction in the marriage.

Sometimes take charge of planning something and deciding when and where to go because they can perceive it as being boring or showing low effort when they have to often initiate plans for the two of you. When you plan it, think about what you would like to do without completely ignoring their preferences.

At times, their likes and preferences can take a backseat to simply adding some excitement to their life, regardless of what the activity is. They know what they like to do, but if they don't get to see what you like to do, it can be unattractive. They may simply enjoy the intrigue and anticipation of having someone else plan something.

They also can be impressed with the thought and effort you put into it. Initiate the event, know how to get there, what to do when there, what to do afterwards. Don't just stop at thinking of something to do and leaving it at that.

In order to allow them the feeling that you are initiating plans but also making sure they have input, you can sometimes present your option as a back-up plan. This is especially good if you really don't have anything specific that you want to do.

For example, you can say, "We can go see the new movie this weekend, but if you have another idea I'm open to hearing about it." This shows them that you are initiating plans to do something together on the weekend but aren't dictating life.

You can do relaxing type of activities that involve non-active things. Things such as cooking together, going for a drive or picnic in a park. These types of things can still be exciting simply because they break up what you would typically do.

You can do physical activities with them. Activities that use a little energy and involve active things, such as walking around a city, hiking, tennis, golf, bowling, skiing. Things that take a little bit of physical activity to get the blood pumping. It creates a different kind of connection to you.

You can do adrenaline inducing activities, such as an amusement park or a sporting event. Some people need spikes in their adrenaline at times. They can't be flat line with their emotions all the time. To them, life is boring if they don't have these occasional spikes or changes to their normal levels.

You can show an adventurous side or even an edgy, risky or daring side of yourself. Your spouse doesn't want danger or trouble in their life, and they definitely don't want anyone's safety to be compromised, but they may want to see something out of the ordinary from you at times. It might appear as impulsive behavior or as a risk taking activity, but really it's just that you are focused on not missing out on potential entertainment while still being safe.

Be careful not to confuse being edgy or daring with being a "party person". Too much of this can take away from the other core components of who you are as an overall person, even if you don't mean to project that perception. Don't over-do trying to be the center of attention all the time.

One important side note – relying on drugs or excessive alcohol use is an unhealthy way of creating fun and excitement. Take the time and effort to find healthy ways of having fun and excitement in life, even if the activity seems more simplistic.

Engaging

"I really liked how talkative you were with everyone tonight!" Tiffany enjoys conversation, but just didn't realize how attractive it can be to her husband for her to verbally interact with other people, even if she doesn't know them very well.

Nick finds it attractive when she actively engages in conversation with someone because it makes him feel good that other people enjoy being around her. He knows she won't do this all the time and that she needs some time alone to feel energized again, but he does like the effort she makes to let this side of herself out at times.

Your spouse wants to see you having fun and enjoying life, by yourself, alone with them and when talking to other people. They love to see you laughing and smiling. Making eye contact with them and with others can be especially important. Showing an engaged personality toward people can be a good thing.

They may want to see your openness in initiating and continuing conversations with other people, as well as with them. They can take pride that other people enjoy being around you too. When you are in a conversation with someone, your spouse gets to sit back and watch your zest for life. How other people view you may have an impact for your spouse.

Letting other people, especially your spouse, see this zest for life can be incredibly appealing. They like to see your energy and enthusiasm, as opposed to being reserved. Even if you're shy, just have open body language to show that you have a vitality about you once they get to know you.

Don't be afraid to introduce yourself to people you don't know. You may sometimes be unsure if a particular person wants to talk to you and get to know you. But the truth is that people usually want to talk to other people. In general, people enjoy meeting others and getting to know them, as long as you aren't invading their privacy, disrespecting them or being rude.

The easiest way to do this is to think of it as a back and forth exchange of what makes each of you distinctive and individualistic. Talk about things you're passionate about or know about. This is where having hobbies, interests, dreams, skills, increasing knowledge and having experiences or adventures is another benefit to you. It gives them an insight into who you are as a person. Show them your world.

On the flip side, ask open-ended questions about them, something they have an interest in, or even what they're wearing. People will talk about themselves fairly easily if it's something they're passionate about. You're trying to find their exclamation point in life. So find what excites them and ask them questions about it. Show an interest in their world.

Third, show an interest in the world itself. You can ask them about common friends that you have. Discuss current world events, sporting events, movies/TV shows that are popular. Compare something happening today with what happened in the past or current trends.

Keeping up to date with these types of things helps you keep conversation going.

Make it amusing for people to talk to you, but don't confuse it with flirting. It's not done to make your spouse feel uncomfortable or jealous. It simply gives your spouse a chance to see other people interested in you as a person, but with the comfort to know that they are the one that gets to build a life with you.

Don't do anything behind your spouse's back or without their full knowledge that you're talking with someone. If your spouse is uncomfortable with your behavior with other people, you may need to change it. Being engaging with people does not mean crossing boundaries your spouse has regarding what is uncomfortable to them.

Playful Banter and Fun Touch

If Jack was honest with himself, chemistry and sexual tension was always a mystery to him. He either had it with someone or he didn't. He obviously had it with Charlotte, but he couldn't explain why. Then he started thinking about what he did with Charlotte which sparked it. He realized it was because he was straight-forward with it. He didn't wait for it to happen.

When they first started dating, he was intent on entertaining each other, laughing and making it known that he liked her and was interested in her. He focused on playful banter, fun touch and forward actions with her. He has continued this approach throughout the marriage. It obviously has worked!

It's the dynamic effort to create a flame and sexual tension outside the bedroom that can help your spouse to feel chemistry with you. They may want you to be aware to generate it at times by having fun, being playful and being a little forward. You are initiating electricity rather than waiting for it to occur, and having a good time while doing it.

Sexual tension and creating a flame is bridging that gap between being a friend to your spouse and being a lover. Remind them that you are both by combining three aspects – being a friend you can talk about anything and laugh with; having random light times with; and being a little brazen with.

Embody some charisma without resorting to adolescent ways of showing your interest in them. Acting immature can be funny sometimes, but often isn't appropriate when you're trying to create heat. Be comfortable around each other, but don't overdo it. The behavior of a teenager, especially during these times, may not be sexy or a turn-on to your spouse.

Use verbal banter with them, both in person and electronically, by using humorous remarks like you would with a friend. Be amusing with them to create a vibrant, lively, spirited dynamic. This is less back and forth questioning and more free-flowing, randomness, joking around and laughing. To use a company metaphor, the dynamic is more like a company summer barbeque and less like a job interview.

You can sometimes mix it up with a different type of exchange. Incorporate a little bit of teasing or sarcasm, without malicious intent, being rude or hurtful. You're exchanging light innocent barbs with each other, similar to what you would do with a buddy or sibling. It's about laughing and in a good-natured way poking fun at a quirk that you find endearing, but not in an insulting or upsetting way.

Banter with them by not being afraid to disagree with them over an opinion or knowledge about something. Keep it light and loose, but still firm on your stance. Don't be insulting, but don't be afraid to get into a back and forth exchange, without expecting them to change their mind on the topic. The ability to effectively get your point across may be attractive.

Other ways to have verbal jabs are to be verbally competitive with some harmless trash talking; find a way to answer a question without actually saying yes or no but still answering it; over exaggerating something in a silly way; making a ludicrous conclusion or comparison to what someone said or what is happening around you; or an alternate meaning to what you know they're saying. Doing it with a smirk or a wink can keep the right tone as well.

Banter can be non-sexual, but don't shy away from making it sexual either. Unlike a friend or sibling, you're reminding them of the status of your relationship, while having levity at the same time. Blend it naturally into the conversation. You're joking and being mischievous without going overboard or being rude.

If your spouse makes a comment that is leaning toward sexy or even an outright sexual joke or comment, roll with it and continue that vein of banter back toward them. Make a sexual joke or comment of your own, while being relaxed and comfortable with it. If it's done in person, using eye contact while doing this can be a good thing too.

Creating chemistry through touch is sticking to the theme of having fun with them and treating them like a friend. This kind of touch and actions should be playful, but tied in with something happening at the moment. Touch their arm while laughing; bump their shoulder while bantering with them; take their hand while walking through a crowd; or touch their back while pointing out something for them to see.

Then mix it up with forward actions that reminds them that you see them as more than just a friend or buddy. Don't only do touch/words that's soft, cautious or overly affectionate. Mix it up with the kind that's more on the firm, brazen or assertive side, but not hurtful and within respectful boundaries.

This boldness can give them affirmation you view them as someone who is irresistible to you, which being too light doesn't always accomplish. One way to do this is to initiate a firm kiss, not rough, that is in between a peck and a make-out session, with your hands securely holding them. Or simply tell them what you are going to do to them sexually later on. Do this during the day then walk away, letting them get on with what they were doing.

Even though you're showing them what kind of relationship you want, it's important to also let the tension build up. You aren't being overly patient about it, but at the same time you aren't forcing it on them. You are showing them that you crave them in a way that isn't satisfied just by being platonic, but letting them decide for themselves without coercion.

Do these kinds of things with words and touch a little at a time, then back off until they're ready for more of what you're giving. Let them process each of your actions one at a time, rather than trying to process too much too soon. A little goes a long way when it comes to sexual tension and building chemistry.

Let this build up throughout the day or week. Show them that your primal passion for them is coming to a boil, but it's not quite there yet.

Your uncontrollable desire for them is reaching its breaking point. They want that primal passionate person inside of you that knows how to control yourself, up until that point where you simply can't control it a minute longer.

Excitement Through Sexual Ravishment

It was off and they both knew it. Skyler and Riley had a great sex life in the beginning, but now it was missing something. After discussing it, they realized they each were missing the same thing from the other – unadulterated passion! They both wanted to feel fire, and maybe even a little lust, from the other one. They wanted to be intensely desired and to let go mentally.

Soft, tender sex is great and needed between them, but often they wanted a little bit of the opposite. More of a "must have you right now, let's let our wild carnal instincts take over and give in to pure unrestrained pleasure." It's the rush of feelings this provides them that softer sex often doesn't provide.

It's an erotic ravishment your spouse feels coming from you that can be attractive to them. They want to feel an animalistic, lustful side between you. They want to feel overcome and overwhelmed with sensations. Show them physically and verbally that you want and crave them so much that you can barely control yourself with sexual passion, but will only do so with their full consent.

Your spouse always reserves the right to decline sexual advances, but they may not want you to tentatively touch them, hesitantly state you're in the mood for sex or to simply ask if they're in the mood for it.

They want you to be more forward when initiating, knowing you will stop if they're not comfortable with it.

They don't just want sex, they want their body consumed by you and your body. That includes from the start of the initiation all the way through to the end, with small breaks in between where they get to consume you and your body. They want to feel the fire you have and to open up their own fire inside of them.

Your forward, brazen actions and words can make them feel intensely desired. You being completely turned on by them, and showing it without reservation, turns them on immensely. Their enjoyment comes both from the pleasure they're feeling and from knowing the effect they're having on you – you're losing your mind with lust because of them.

When doing this, it can feel good to them to turn off their brain for a while and just respond with their instincts and their body. This allows them to mindlessly get lost in the moment and the excitement of the passion. They want to naturally respond to what you do or say, rather than having to decide what to do or being asked by you what action should be taken.

To mentally let go, their preference might be for you to guide the interaction, and to simply follow your words/actions. They trust you to take control during sex if they feel you will be focused on making it a shared pleasurable experience focusing on each others' desires. Make it feel like you have a plan for both of you to be fulfilled, then go about it with an assertive confidence.

Here are some ways to lead like this with ravished passion, with fuller descriptions below. 1) passionately kiss them and press your body weight against theirs; 2) ravish their body with your hands/mouth; 3) take your time; 4) use a variety of speed; 5) gently move them around or lightly hold them in place; 6) grip their hair without hurting them; 7) be verbal about what you're enjoying or what you want them to do.

Passionately kiss them like your life depended on it at that moment, but without being overly wild or out of control with it. While kissing, they may like your hand behind their head, cupping their face or firmly on their lower back. They may like your body weight against theirs, pressed against a wall or on the bed.

Ravish their body like it's the most perfect one you've ever laid eyes on. Use a little bit of firm pressure with your hands, but being very careful not to hurt them. They may like to feel your hands or mouth all over them, exploring every inch. Kiss different parts of their body to gauge their reaction. Use your hands on both their body and your own.

Take your time and be in control of your actions. You want to extend the enjoyment for both of you as long as possible. Getting to an orgasm or to certain sexual acts can be a buildup where you are both ready to explode if it doesn't happen. This also allows you to listen to their verbal or non-verbal clues of what they are wanting from you. But don't ignore how important having their orgasm can be to them.

Add variety of speed to the sexual encounter. You can go slow and sensual, then change it to fast and raw. Alternate between these paces at times. Make them wonder what will come next. Show this different energy and rhythm during all parts of the sexual act. It's a way to keep it active, as well as keeping their senses engaged.

Let loose. If you want to do something, do it. Listen to them and don't continue doing it if they're uncomfortable, but don't hold back either. This is where you may really have to let your primal, uninhibited side out in both words and actions, and to encourage their primal, uninhibited side to come out too.

Move them around, or yourself, when you feel you want to in the moment. This can mean sliding them toward you, turning them to a different position or moving your own body, even if it's just a small shift. Change positions to feel different stimulation, instead of passively waiting for them to suggest it.

When moving them, don't hurt them but keep in mind that they aren't fragile either. You can use your hands, legs or knees to adjust their entire body or just a limb. When you are playfully deliberate about this, it can show them that you're pursuing your own desires, which can be a turn on to them. Remember that it's a balance of pursuing your desires while not ignoring theirs.

They may also enjoy you holding them in place, being careful that they are okay with how you do it. You can lightly grip their hands, wrists, waist or back. Liking the sensation of being in place does not mean overuse of force. Meaning they may enjoy being held down, but when they try to move, let up so they can.

You can run a hand up the back of their neck and head, then gently move their head using the hair close to their scalp. It's more of a firm hair grip than hair pulling that can hurt. It has to be done soft enough so you don't cause pain, but also gives them that feeling of a sudden urge coming over you. This can be done either when they are facing you or away from you.

Be verbal with words, moans or just sounds. They may want verification that they're bringing you joy or that they're affecting you in a good way. They may want to hear what you find stimulating or to compliment their body. Let them know how much you like it and what you like about it. Your words might be about them, but really what they want to know is how much they are turning you on.

They may wish for you to tell them what you want them to do. They want to know you're receiving pleasure, but specifically that what they do is a key source of that pleasure. This is where you telling them what you want and desire is sexy to them. Be careful with this, but they also might want you to sound a little commanding with it or to say things to them you wouldn't say outside of the bedroom.

Emphasize what they're doing right that you want to continue, not what they're doing wrong. Positive affirmations can be very helpful when they are unsure about something. Praise them when they attempt to do something outside their comfort zone or trying something different, even their small efforts.

Use a combination. One of the most effective things to do is to use several of these tactics at the same time. For example, lean your weight against them, hold their hands with yours above their head, kiss their neck and have your leg softly but firmly rubbing between their legs. It's the combination of sensations, as well as your assertiveness to take charge, that will have their mind spinning.

Don't forget to laugh and have fun during sex. Do research in order to change up your routine. This includes both foreplay and overall technique. It never hurts to constantly be learning, even in the bedroom, and to stay out of a boring routine. Take your time to learn what they enjoy before going too far and trying to do too much, too soon.

Really understand what they want. The more you enthusiastically focus on what they want and desire, the more likely they are to reciprocate with what you most want and desire. This is particularly true for the things you don't quite understand why they would like something, as long as it doesn't go against your morals.

Talk to your spouse about what they're comfortable with and is a turn on to them. Get their acknowledgement that they are okay with certain actions or certain words, and that you will stop if they are not in the mood for it. An important aspect of consent is about getting their permission of what behavior, touch and words are acceptable to them. This is a must.

Action Plan for "Be Full of Life" quality

Show your fun side of being carefree and letting loose.

Live in the moment:
- Be carefree, vibrant and turn the mind off.
- Embrace fun, excitement and enjoyment.

Engaging:
- Be vibrant and engaging with direct eye contact.
- Introduce yourself and talk with people.

Playful Banter and Fun Touch:
- Use playful banter, fun touch and forward actions.
- Bridge the gap between being friends and being lovers.

Excitement through sexual ravishment:
- Show your primal craving for them with passion.
- Guide the interaction to let them let go mentally.

Chapter 6

Independent Quality #5

Be Self-Fulfilling

Let Them Show Their Interest Too

It was normal. It felt like their usual day to day process. Jordan would pursue Denise and she would either accept or rebuff that pursuit. It was everything from trying to make physical contact with her, to telling her how beautiful she was, to making sexual advances. In a sense, she really liked it because she didn't have to worry about his attention to her.

But another part of her didn't like it because she felt like he was being needy, a little smothering and using her as a crutch. He gave the impression that he felt complete only when he pursued her and she accepted because he would pout or become agitated when she didn't.

In addition, she wanted to be the one to pursue or show signs of interest in him once in a while. She wanted to feel like she set her sights on Jordan to get his attention and have the thrill of him responding to her efforts.

Being self-fulfilling means that you are not depending on your spouse's presence or attention for how fulfilled or content you are in life. When you push too hard for your spouse's time or attention, it can give them the impression you are dependent on them in a non-healthy manner and that you need their presence to feel content.

Back off to show them you can feel fulfilled with yourself when needed, rather than making them feel guilty to provide this fulfillment for you. In addition, it will give them an opportunity to pursue your time and attention, which may be an attractive thing for them to do. They may want to do these things toward you and get a little boost of ego when you respond back to them.

Think about how often you seek their attention, flirt with them, casually touch them, compliment them often, initiate a lot of the talking, make suggestive remarks or hover around them. If you over-do these things, it doesn't give them the chance to do these things toward you first.

You have to balance being the pursuer and being pursued by your spouse. Balance showing your interest in them and letting them signal their interest in you. Balance showing that you crave them with giving them the room to show they crave you.

One of the reasons this balance may be important to them is because it's a way of showing desire toward you equally with being desired by you. When they make the effort and you reciprocate that effort, they get that feeling of being wanted and desired because they have something beneficial to offer you not just because they happen to be there. They can see that when they make an effort for your attention, you find them interesting, intellectually stimulating, fun and sexy.

They still enjoy the fun of pursuing you and trying for your attention when you aren't constantly making an effort for theirs. They get a thrill when you respond back to their attention-getting enticements. If you are always vying for their attention either verbally or physically, they can forget how fun it is to vie for yours and the excitement of you noticing their effort to attract you.

For Denise, Jordan going overboard with his infatuation for her or his attraction to her is nice, but it didn't give her that opportunity to attract him. Being the one to try to attract him can be fun for her to do occasionally. When all she has to do is "exist" to get his focus and attention, it takes away some of the fun and specialness for her because she feels any woman could "exist" for him.

Your spouse may be used to you making advances toward them. So, they may not think to make advances toward you, like when you two were first dating. They may miss that aspect of their own personality at times. They may not have been as bold about it as you were in pursuing them, but they enticed you and let you know they were interested in their own way.

To them, pursuing you may simply mean doing and saying things to show an interest in being pursued by you. Some people are uncomfortable being called a pursuer, but we all pursue by doing little things to show that we are open to receiving someone's attention. Showing an interest in being pursued is also being a pursuer.

Watch for your spouse's signals of interest. They may not pursue the way you do or show their signal of interest the way you do. It may be a lot more subtle than your way, but it doesn't mean it's wrong. If you miss those signals, you could be hurting your chances of a passionate connection.

While you don't want to ignore your spouse's initial sign of pursuing, don't jump at it either. Give a little response back to them, but don't go overboard. Show you're paying attention to what they're doing, but you really want to have fun of going back and forth a little with each other pursuing. This is more rewarding to them than just jumping at their first overture, like you're desperately waiting for it.

Some people don't pursue their spouse's attention through verbal means. Some do it through their actions. It may be when they put effort into feeling unique to you and you recognize and appreciate this. For example, they spend hours to find just the right outfit for a special occasion to look good for you or look through dozens of birthday cards to find the one that says just the right thing.

From a physical standpoint, your spouse may have a hard time verbally or overtly physically initiating touch, even though they may want to. They may "initiate" in other ways that are not verbal or physical. Talk with them about how they feel comfortable initiating, and then pick up those clues they give you.

However, this doesn't mean never giving them any attention or flirting at all. You do need to give some because this may be a desire of theirs. You need to strike the right balance between the two. You need to give it when they are flirting or giving you attention. You just can't drown them in it non-stop.

It's giving them the ability to be in control of their own flirting, the fun of attracting you and the joy of knowing that they can still get your attention despite how long you've been together. It gives them a chance to entice you and feel the joy of you responding back. This is a great benefit, they feel good when they want to get your attention and are successful in that goal.

Build Anticipation, Create Desire for Connection

"I can't wait to get there!" Seth had a strange sense of wanting to rush home to be with Elizabeth. He couldn't understand why. He always liked being around her, but this was different. He had gotten up early in the morning before she was awake and left for work. Then he had met a friend for happy hour after work.

Elizabeth had been incredibly busy all day as well and they didn't have time to talk or communicate at all. This was very unusual. She almost always reached out to him during the day, but when she didn't today, it created a desire in him to rush home to her.

Build anticipation of being together and create a desire for connection by being apart sometimes. There is an excitement of coming back together when you're not constantly around each other. Anticipation of being together can be a very powerful emotion. It creates a desire to connect with that person.

You can help your spouse to create this connection and longing to be near you. There is a fine line between paying attention to them and smothering them or looking clingy to them. They want time with you, but then they may want you to give space at times.

It creates a longing for them toward you and intensity of wanting your attention, your presence and your engagement again. It creates a back and forth dance in which they can create their own engagement with you. This includes both space outside of the house and giving them space by doing your own thing while at home.

Sometimes it's not physical space, sometimes it's verbal space or sometimes it's emotional space. It's letting them go at a pace they're comfortable with and without giving them guilt or whining about an unmet desire of yours.

When you're apart, it can be exciting and thrilling when you come back together. It can be exciting and thrilling not knowing exactly when you will be back together. That anticipation can be exhilarating. They look forward to seeing you again when you're not there.

This also means time apart electronically. Don't purposely avoid them, but just make sure to keep communication distance occasionally to simulate you two missing each other and wanting to be physically together again soon. A little bit of communication distance occasionally can be very beneficial for both of you, but without overdoing it.

Emotional space is their feeling of having their own personal space and breathing room, which can be as important as physical or verbal space apart. Note that there is a difference between being emotionally distant and simply giving them a little emotional space on occasion.

When Seth acts like or says he wants some space or time apart, that is exactly what Elizabeth gives him. When he is acting frustrated toward her, space and time apart is a good thing to give him. Trying to force him to change his feelings will only result in upsetting him more and does not build his attraction toward her.

However, that doesn't mean overdoing it or going against your spouse's values. Too much time apart can go against their values, so you must be ready to balance the two together. It doesn't do any good to meet one need while destroying another need of theirs.

Another way to give them some space is when they are actively being distant. It can be easy to think they are pulling away from you on purpose or something you did. But the reason may simply be they are busy, sad or stressed about something. Give them some time to sort it out without trying to force them to be near you, either physically or electronically.

If you force this or make them feel guilty about the way they are acting, you could make them more stressed and make it worse between the two of you. If they feel you will give them space when they need it, they may be willing to come back closer to you in a quicker timeframe. Don't sabotage your own need by pressuring them or making them feel guilty.

Let Them Help and Impress Too

Carrie was always very dependable. It was one of the reasons that Ron fell in love with her. But after several years of marriage, that dependability just felt different. It was almost like she was constantly trying to impress him or show how valuable she is to him. Like her normal, regular attributes weren't enough to impress him.

From his viewpoint, she was starting to feel more like a servant who felt she had to say yes to everything and couldn't ask anything from him to help or to impress her. It was a very unsettling feeling for Ron.

Don't get caught up in constantly trying to impress your spouse. They want to impress you as well. It can make them feel good to help and impress you at times. It's another way of them having good self-esteem and can be thrilling to them when they do this for you. Remember that there should be an equal balance of effort between two people in a relationship.

Without realizing it, you can come across to them as being too eager to please, trying too hard and looking desperate for their approval or acceptance to always see you a certain way. While you may think this is being nice to your spouse, they may see it as being servant-like and unattractive. It can come across as the opposite of independence and individuality.

They want a partner, not a servant. When you're a servant, you drop everything the second your spouse needs something, regardless of what you're doing at the time. When you're a partner, you are there for your spouse when they really need you, but you won't unfairly or unnecessarily rearrange your life because of it.

Your spouse doesn't expect you to do every little thing they ask of you. You may think they would be upset if you decline their requests. But they usually won't be upset because they never expected 100% compliance. That would be you acting like a pushover in their mind. In addition, they may not realize they are being unthoughtful or even lazy with their request. Sometimes they just need a gentle reminder.

They also never expect you to agree with every opinion they have. They want to know you have your own opinions, thoughts and values. Those things don't always have to align with theirs.

If Ron's request doesn't fit well with Carrie's time frame or what she's doing, he is usually okay with her saying "no" during those times. He doesn't want to feel guilty that she's completely rearranging her life for him. Feeling guilty turns him off and he starts to feel bad about himself. He doesn't want her to say no to him all the time, but at times it is alright with him.

You must strike the right balance between the extremes of doing everything for them and completely ignoring them. The balance between hovering around them and never being at home. The balance between needlessly apologizing for things that aren't your fault and never apologizing at all when you are wrong. They need to know that you are there for them but aren't there to do everything for them.

If you are always trying to fix their problems for them, you may be trying to overly impress them and trying too hard to be their hero. It's good to impress your spouse, but sometimes you need to back off and understand that they are capable of fixing their own problems.

Don't assume that all the things you do will make them happy, make them feel connected to you or motivated to meet your needs later. Often you may end up doing a dozen different things for them, hoping one or two will hit the target bullseye and make them feel good and feel happy. This tactic usually doesn't work for creating a close connection.

The point is not to randomly do a dozen different things, but to narrow it down to doing those specific things that actually do make a difference in their happiness, make them feel closer to you and to want to meet your needs in return.

The way you do this is to listen to their requests and even ask them what specific things will accomplish this goal. Doing a variety of different things hoping it will make them happy makes you look needy and desperate. This has the opposite effect of what you were hoping to accomplish.

It is okay to ask favors of your spouse on occasion. Ask them to do something for you, but make sure it's something you legitimately need help with, not just you being lazy. Most people would feel short-changed if they never get to show effort to their spouse, and then have that effort acknowledged and reciprocated back to them.

This includes letting them do things for you when they offer or make a sacrifice for you. Don't fight it because equal effort means you both deserve the same good treatment. Both of you should give equally to the relationship. Don't give the impression that either one of you is on a higher level than the other.

It's a show of healthy self-esteem when you expect equal effort on both sides of a relationship. Letting them do things for you is a way they see equal effort in the marriage. When you don't let them do things for you, even if you're trying to be nice, it creates an unequal balance in their mind and is a turn off for them.

This might be one way they are showing that they are making an effort toward you. Remember, their way of making an effort for you may look different than your way of making an effort toward them. Part of them feeling unique and special to you is when they offer to do little things for you. It's a mistake when you say no to these little offerings by them.

This can be partially their way of giving you attention. If they are coming to you, doing something for you and giving you attention, don't shoot them down. If you shoot them down, they will stop this form of giving attention, as well as more obvious ways you do enjoy. You could be denying your own needs in the future without even realizing it.

Doing something for you has another benefit for them. It allows them to stop their racing thoughts for a while. Some people have a hard time turning their mind off from all the events and stresses of life. Focusing on doing something for someone else allows them to fully relax their mind in a way they can't do otherwise.

Take Charge of Your Own Happiness

Ashley and Quinn finally understood what it was like for each of them to control their own happiness. For so long, they both felt that the other one was in control of it, depending on whether or not their spouse did what was important to them.

They were both getting frustrated when their spouse wouldn't do what was important to them. They were hedging on truly enjoying life based on what the other one was giving and it was making both of them unhappy. But they wanted to change from their spouse controlling their happiness to controlling it themselves.

So they did two things. First, they assessed if they both were doing what was important and appealing to the other one. Second, they both stated the type of marriage they wanted to be in and was important to them without demanding their spouse do it or suggesting their spouse was wrong for what they were doing instead. Based on how their spouse reacts to this information, Ashley and Quinn then decide what to do to make themselves happy.

Take desperation for something out of your decisions in life because you can unknowingly make bad choices during these times. For instance, know what you want in the marriage, but don't be desperate for it in your mind. You have to find fulfillment within yourself and let other things or other people add to that fulfillment, not be the basis of it or the basis of your existence / happiness.

When you're not happy with something in the marriage, you have to guard against making it seem like you're putting your happiness in your spouse's hands. You can't sit around being unhappy and waiting for them to someday do what's fulfilling to you. You have to be in charge of your own happiness. But how you go about doing this is what makes a difference.

There's a question to ask yourself about balancing being accommodating to them and being accommodated by them. Why would you want to accommodate someone that doesn't want to accommodate you equally? Don't let hurting someone be normalized. This is both for pain you're causing them and pain they're causing you. The pain and hurt will continue until you stand up to it and not accept it.

You must tell yourself that you are deserving of your spouse being head over heels for you and will do what's meaningful to you. If you're not getting that feeling from them, it might be a sign to step back to reassess what you want your marriage to be like and how much you value yourself to be deserving of that.

State what is important to you, but don't make a demand to your spouse that they do it. You can state your desires but not that they have a responsibility to do it. They get to decide whether or not to do it, regardless of how important it is to you. But, you then get to decide if that's the kind of relationship you want and if their actions suitably match up with this.

This distinction is important. While you aren't owed anything in marriage, you do have a right to say what type of marriage you want to be in. So instead of giving ultimatums or telling them they must do something, change your stance to simply letting them know what type of relationship you're striving for.

But stay happy doing this to reinforce to yourself that you are in control of your happiness. Don't allow the situation to control your mood, or fall into being vindictive or pouting. Essentially, you're in control of your life, how you deal with it and being content with it.

It's then up to them if they can accommodate what you want or not. If they can't accommodate that, they are not bad. They're just simply looking for different qualities in a partner than what you're looking for in a partner. Don't give an order, judge them for what they are doing or insinuate they are wrong. Just acknowledge that each of you have different ways you want to live your life.

They are not wrong in what they're doing, but you also are not wrong in wanting what's important to you. Don't make them feel guilty and don't let them make you feel guilty. Sometimes what each of you desire just aren't compatible together. That's the decision you have to make and it's a decision of what you want to convey to them after this realization.

Depending on your beliefs and values, you may or may not feel comfortable saying that the two of you might not be right for each other or aren't compatible together. That is up to you, your morals and what you believe in. That's a personal decision only you can make. Definitely seek counseling before making any decisions because the long-term emotional toll can be extensive.

But first, make sure to explore all qualities of what your spouse finds attractive and important to them because you may hit on one thing that inspires them to want to meet your needs and desires differently than they have in the past.

It's really important not to rush into any life altering decisions. Take a step back to assess your own actions and behavior. Remember that sometimes your actions can cause their reactions, either good or bad. It's easy to just assume you've tried everything to make the marriage work, but sometimes you can be blind to how your attitude influences them and their attitude.

Sometimes you can do a couple of things that get their attention and get them to see you in a little different light. Then you do one additional thing, either an Independent quality or Team quality, that really connects with them to inspire them to do what's important to you and find attractive. Even when it seems bleak, there is always potential to inspire them in a positive manner.

Action Plan for "Be Self-Fulfilling" quality

Show you don't need their attention or approval for how fulfilled and content you are in life.

Let them show their interest too:

- ⊙ Back off to let them show their interest in you.
- ⊙ When they do, respond back without being clingy.

Build anticipation, create desire for connection:

- ⊙ Build anticipation by being apart at times.
- ⊙ Create a longing with physical, verbal space at times.

Let them help and impress too:

- ⊙ Be comfortable asking for a favor from them occasionally.
- ⊙ Don't be afraid to say no when they ask for something.

Take charge of your own happiness:

- ⊙ Don't let either of you feel guilty for your desires.
- ⊙ Tell them what kind of marriage you want to be in.

Section Three

The Team Qualities

Show your good-natured, caring or attentive partnership style, being flexible and focused on fulfilling your spouse's desires.

The five Team qualities show you adore your spouse and are crazy about them in a way they can truly feel. These are five ways to show you cherish them to give what they want and fulfill their desires, not just what you want to give. It's thinking about what makes them feel the most united with you. The five Team qualities are:

Be Supportive

Be Uplifting

Be Easy Going

Be Enticing

Be Affectionate

As you go through this section, determine two things. Which quality do you find most attractive when your spouse displays it? Which quality does your spouse find most attractive when you display it? Then do the actions listed to fulfill those things for each other.

The Attraction Quiz at the end of the book can also help you and your spouse identify the quality most important to each of you.

Chapter 7

Team Quality #1

Be Supportive

Let Them Express Their Feelings

Kate just came home from her usual stressful day at work. She starts venting to Justin about the day – her manager is still on her case about the project that should be done soon; her co-worker is not being cooperative; and to top it off, "you wouldn't believe the attitude the store cashier gave me on the way home. Eye rolling and maybe even a sneer was involved!"

Justin couldn't understand this nightly ritual of hers. He had all the same issues, but he didn't see the need to spill out his frustrations about them. For Kate though, it was very cathartic. She always seemed to be in a better mood if she was able to do this for about half an hour and for him to just listen to her.

At times, your spouse may have a need to vent and release their stress, worries, problems and frustrations. Something very important and attractive to your spouse could be to simply have you listen whole-heartedly when they express their feelings and emotions, acknowledge how they feel or simply offer a hug.

They may need to vent their feelings and emotions so they can get those things out of their system. Simply the feeling of being listened to by you may be one way they deal with and release stress in their life. They may not want you to say too much, other than acknowledging that you are hearing what they say, but not making suggestions or critiquing what they could do.

At times they just want to unload their thoughts in a way that doesn't make sense to you. It's not necessarily them being unhappy, unreasonable or ungrateful. They just need to do this without you ignoring them, thinking it's unimportant, taking an opposite stance or trying to fix the issue for them.

When you disagree, take the opposite stance or question something they say, you end up making the subject and focus about yourself rather than them. Sometimes just let them talk about it and ask questions how they feel about it, without trying to make it about how you feel or what you think they should do.

As an example, say they start talking about a difficult special project at work. You may be thinking they want to quit their job or are blaming something in their life for it. You may not give your full attention or say they shouldn't feel that way, instead of just listening or offering physical comfort.

When you do that, they can get frustrated with you because they just needed to vent for a few minutes and then they would feel better by you simply hearing what they say. They are hurt and maybe feeling lonely because you won't just simply listen to them.

Practice being silent for a moment before you say anything so that you can really try to feel what they are saying and simply that you support them. At times, they can say something in a worse way than they mean to. It's better not to say anything for a little while than to say the wrong thing back to them. Be able to put aside your own feelings and emotions for a moment in order to listen to them.

Acknowledge and support their feelings, even if you don't always agree with the words they're using. Sometimes you may need to separate their words from their feelings because the two may not always be in sync with one another.

Sometimes they're just making an off-hand comment that they don't really need you to respond. In fact, if you respond, it may create a disagreeable feeling or reaction from them. They just want to do a quick unload of their feelings and don't expect you to say anything in return.

If they ask a question of you, a simple yes or no from you is also advisable at times. Over-explaining or over-apologizing unnecessarily may create a back and forth volley between the two of you that doesn't really help the situation. Communication is important, but there are times when fewer words are better communication than multiple words.

They have a right to their emotions. If the emotions are directed at you, you can acknowledge that they have a right to feel that way, even if you don't completely understand or agree with them. If you don't agree with them, you can at least show that the issue is important to them, so therefore it's important to you. You can't hold this against them, even if those emotions are about you.

Realize that defending yourself can be an automatic instinct of yours when they come to you with a problem or request. The instinct can be to verbally push back, invalidate it and try to make them feel that it shouldn't be an issue at all. Instead, what they want is for you to see why they would be upset about it.

When they bring up something that frustrates them, instead of giving a reason why you do something, ask them questions about their frustration. Ask them to give a couple of specific examples so you can understand it better. Ask them if this is a one-time event or something they feel a lot.

If they ask for your opinion about a problem or a decision they have to make, it's easy to tell them what they should do based on your preferences. But they may want you to ask them questions to get them to see what they should do based on their preferences.

Such as, what are the pros and cons of each option? What is the likely outcome of each option? Is there another option they haven't thought of? How will it affect other people?

Kate doesn't always know exactly what she wants on a certain issue or concern until she has talked about it out loud. She feels better when she processes her feelings and emotions through words. Talking about it is often how she processes what action she is really seeking.

Your spouse will let you know specifically if they want some action to be taken by you or a solution offered. Even though they often just want you to listen, there will be times when they're specifically asking for action to be taken. You can't get complacent that they are always just releasing emotions and feelings. You must specifically listen for those times and ask if they are looking for something to be done by you.

Another way to support their feelings is to hear what they're trying to tell you, even if they're not using words to do it. Take yourself out of the situation or what you want the outcome to be. Slow everything down – your mind, your emotions and your agenda.

Sometimes the hardest thing to do is to take your expectations out of the equation, but that may be the most helpful thing to do for them. Really try to understand what they're going through and what they need at the moment. This can't be emphasized enough – truly turn off your expectations, put yourself in their shoes and understand what they are needing.

Having expectations for what's important to you and makes you happy is healthy. However, where you have to be careful is having expectations, or your own agenda, for their life that doesn't involve your happiness. It's okay to want the best for them, but you have to support them by removing any insinuations of what they should be doing with their life. This pressure may be overwhelming to them.

Two-Way Conversations and Support Interests

Brad loves talking about fishing. Claire had no idea the subject could be as involved as it is. She is often tempted to cut him off when he starts talking about it because she has very little interest in it, except when he cooks one for dinner. However, she knows better than to do that because it makes Brad feel closer to her when he is able to have conversations with her about what he's passionate for.

Your spouse may have a need to engage in conversations as a way to bond with you. This is more than just an exchange of what makes each of you distinctive and interesting. They can be attracted to the emotions that come from the back and forth talking and your complete attention during this time. This involves not only talking about each of your interests, but also talking about mundane, everyday things as well.

There are three good ways to show you are interested in what they have to say. 1) Take a breath between sentences to see if they have a response to what you've said. 2) Talk about subjects they are interested in and be interactive by asking questions. 3) Don't steer something back to be about you, try to be the center of attention by talking too much or interrupt them too much – allow the spotlight to be on them sometimes.

This is how they may feel close to you and a deep connection with you, especially with things they enjoy talking about. The expressing of ideas, feelings and emotions through conversation needs to flow out of them for both a physical release and an emotional connection. It's likely also important to them to hear you talk about things going on in your life.

Every verbal interaction doesn't have to be detailed, in depth, and time consuming. They just want to know that you are making the effort to stay connected to them through verbal communication, are thinking about them and taking an interest in their life.

This is also how they feel valued to you, when you're willing to talk and listen to them at any time. Similar to when you want to do some other activity and appreciate it when they are adaptable to you with your activity, they may want to have conversations and appreciate it when you are adaptable to them with talking.

It can be easy for you to make fun of or dismiss your spouse's believes, hobbies and interests that you don't care about, rather than having a conversation about those things. When you do that, you are making fun of or dismissing part of them as a person. You don't have to adopt those things for yourself, but at least talk about those things and show that you support and care about all parts of them as a person.

Don't make them feel as though the things they like are stupid. This only accomplishes to make them either angry for a hurtful comment or make them feel guilty and insecure about the things they like. It's not up to you to decide what activities they should and should not be interested in.

Take an interest in their dreams and goals. Not only listen to your spouse talk about them, but also ask about them. This may mean you need to do some research on those subjects. Know some details about those things to talk about them. Fully support those dreams and goals, even if it's not a goal or dream of yours. Listen to them when they want to tell you something, even if it's not a subject you would normally bring up yourself.

Claire gives Brad support to do what makes him happy. A lot of times she may not understand it and fully appreciate how something can make him happy, but the worst thing she can do is to try to limit the happiness he derives from it. She refrains from making any hurtful comments about it and watches how it puts a smile on his face.

Once you stop trying to limit those things of importance to them, you may start to encourage them to do things that are important to them and make them happy. To have a happy marriage, you both need to be happy and part of that comes from doing things that you derive happiness from. The one exception you can make to this is when it comes to the financial aspect of these hobbies. Remember that spending excessive money and getting into debt problems can be a problem in marriage.

Just as important as listening to them, talk to your spouse about things in your life. Hearing about your day at work or what your dreams and desires are makes them feel close to you. Much like you may feel close to them when your physical bodies are close, they may feel close to you when words are close and flowing back and forth.

99

Recognize this may be one of the ways for them to bond with you. Don't make fun of this or push it off as being unimportant. They may really want this type of back and forth conversation. Tell them what's going on in your head and life.

When you are having this type of conversation, make it interactive. It's important for them to know what's going in with you and your life, but they also want a chance to interject with their thoughts about it too.

Thoughtful Acts

Matt smelled them before he saw them. Fresh baked cookies were his favorite indulgence. He and Megan both did chores in the household, but one thing Megan knew – she was in charge of the cookies. To Matt, making a fresh batch of cookies was one of the best things she could do for him, similar to how much she loves his homemade cheese dip. It made him incredibly happy and truly motivated him to do nice things for her as well.

Doing things around the house in the way they like it being done could be a big factor for your spouse and what they find attractive. It's not just that you take initiative to do household things or what's on the to-do list to show you're self-sufficient. It's that you work with them to determine what they really get out of your efforts and how you can accommodate them better as a team.

For example, you both agree that the dishwasher needs to be loaded and unloaded periodically. They may think it should be done right away, so dishes don't sit in the sink. You may think differently, so you need to discuss why their timeframe is important to them and how this gesture affects them.

Work with your spouse to see which of you doesn't mind doing certain chores or things to do. Work together on these issues. One person may not mind doing one of these items, but dislikes doing something else. This can include things like cooking, doing the grocery shopping, sweeping or doing laundry.

Cooking may be a particularly attractive quality to your spouse, but it's not just the act of cooking. It's the compassion of finding out what they like to eat and providing it for them. It's the time, effort and love you put into what they find appetizing and makes them happy. This is similar to the time, effort and love of what you like them to do toward you.

Being thoughtful can be about helping them out in various little ways in life. Matt makes Megan's favorite beverage in the morning and cleans out her car for her. She is beyond grateful to him for these small things because she hates doing them herself.

Supporting them with gestures can simply mean remembering small details about them. Remember what type of drink they like. Remember what their favorite desert is. Noticing small details about their life can mean a lot to them.

Small acts of thoughtfulness are reminders that you're thinking about your spouse. It can be something as simple as buying flowers, making them a card or asking if they need anything when you go to the grocery store. It could be something tangible they can hold and look at to remind them that you are thinking about them. Or it could be non-tangible like holding the door open for them.

A good start to thoughtful acts is to think about their senses. What do they like to taste? What music do they like to listen to? What feels good on their skin? What appeals to their eyes? What fragrance do they like to smell? What affects their instinctual sixth sense of what a caring person does, such as running an errand for them?

A lot of this comes down to doing specific things for your spouse because you know they like it. It's not just a benefit to them, it's a benefit to you too. When you do a specific act that they truly appreciate, it encourages them to reciprocate back to you with what you truly appreciate. As long as you're getting this reciprocation, you're not being a doormat at all.

Your spouse may want different types of things from you to show them that you truly care about them. It may be something very simple that you wouldn't really think would make such a big impact on them. This is where action on your part can make them feel better, even if it's done in a way you normally wouldn't.

The person making the request is the one who decides when a request has been met, not the person who is providing it. Too often, you may do things for them thinking that what you were doing was enough. But it might not be done in the way that meets that need of theirs. You may be meeting their requests in the way that fulfills you, not them.

For example, they ask you to cook a new dish for dinner. You cooked the new dinner recipe but made it very spicy. You knew that they don't care for spicy foods, but you wanted to try the dinner that way anyway. You were fulfilling their request in the way you wanted to do it, not in the way that would please and fulfill them. You were meeting their request to cook the dinner but fulfilled the request in the way that you would be fulfilled by.

You may claim that you were meeting their request and doing it for them so you can avoid feeling guilty about cooking it your way. Your defensiveness can turn to anger toward them for not appreciating the fact that you cooked the meal they requested. So, on top of not getting their request met, you get mad at them when they expressed that they didn't appreciate your effort.

It is okay for you to try out a new recipe that is spicy, and that you know you would enjoy more than your spouse would. But you shouldn't do it on the night that they are making a specific request for a specific dinner. Instead, wait for another night to cook the recipe in a spicy way and acknowledge that you're really doing it this way for yourself and for your need, not for them.

You may think that when you have a valid reason to deny your spouse's need, want or desire, that it's over at that point. However, ignoring their concern or their longing for something doesn't make it disappear. It stays as frustration, de-motivates them to meet your needs later and is a sign to them that you're not supporting them.

A lot of times, you may try to think of why you can't do something they ask of you. Some of the "why's" sound legitimate, especially the ones that deal with your own self-esteem and insecurity issues. But there is one thing that you may notice. No matter how legitimate your "why" is at the time, it rarely makes their needs and desires go way.

They may stop asking for something after being turned down numerous times, but it is always still there in the back of their mind because they are being denied something that is important to them. It hurts the marriage because that longing of theirs doesn't go away – it just gets replaced with frustration and hurt.

Take Turns and Compromise

They couldn't believe they were at this impasse again. Jake wanted to watch his weekly sports game at the same time Brianna wanted to go out together to a specific weekly music event held at the same time. "Can't she see how I need to unwind with sports from a stressful week?" "Can't he see how important it is for me to go out one night a week together to a music event?"

Jake realized he had to be better at compromising, so a compromise of taking turns became the solution. One week they would watch the sports game he enjoyed. The next week, they would go out to do the music activity she enjoyed. Both of them are doing things that aren't their favorite thing to do, but both are also getting to do things that are their favorite to do. This was hard for Jake to do sometimes, but he knew it was necessary.

A major area of conflict happens when you both want to do something at the same time. You want to do one thing together and your spouse wants to do something else at the same time together. This conflict may happen often because everyone has their own preferences.

To avoid this conflict, take turns doing one person's activity one time and the other person's activity the next time. Whenever you have conflicting needs at the same time, try to find a way to fulfill both requests, but at different times. Don't default to thinking that only one competing need could be met, which would lead to a big disagreement over it. Instead, stop to think about how one person's activity can be done on a different day or time from the other person's.

When you want to do something, strike a balance to include their need within yours. Don't be stuck on doing everything regarding what you want exactly your way. Doing that makes it very difficult for your spouse to want to fulfill your desires.

If it's not feasible to take turns, you can compromise where each of you get most of what you desire. One helpful thing is to define what each of you are trying to achieve with your desire. Not the request itself, but the result of that request being fulfilled. Once you define each other's result, the request itself might change because you may find a different way to achieve that result.

Jake's desired result was watching sports games with Brianna because he enjoyed sports and wanted to spend time with her. Brianna's desired result was going out to dinner with Jake to spend time with him outside of the house dressed up. They don't do this every time, but the compromise they made was to go to a restaurant that had a sports game on. It's a good compromise when there's a game that Jake really wants to watch and when they can still have a good discussion either before or after the game.

The hardest part of compromise is coming to the realization that on a certain issue you can get some of what you want, but not all of it. On difficult issues, list out what your minimum requirements are for that situation and what their minimums are. Then try to find the compromise where you both at least get your minimum requirements met.

Compromise also means that you each of you may have to lean towards the middle. For example, if one spouse is a saver with money while the other is more of a spender, both can meet toward the middle when there are issues with these differing styles.

The saver may cling to being that way because the other spouse is such a spender, and the same goes for the other spouse. People are naturally the way they are, but are often even more that way when they feel they have to over-compensate for their spouse being the opposite.

So if the saver spouse leaned toward the middle of being a little more loose with money while not completely being free-spirited with it, the spender spouse would feel less of a need to be that way so much and could lean toward being more of a saver.

Another classic example is with chores. For instance, if you want the home to be vacuumed once a week and your spouse is okay with once a month, compromise half way between each spouse's preferred timing. Neither of you gets exactly what you want, but both can be satisfied enough with the outcome.

But it only works when you both strictly adhere to your end of the compromise without cheating. Another compromise is to find out why your spouse isn't doing something you want, instead of just telling them to do it or getting upset at them. For example, say they aren't doing the laundry when they said they would.

Maybe they would prefer doing a different chore and you do the laundry. Maybe they want you to be more flexible to let them do the laundry in a different timeframe than you want. Maybe you're not doing something that is important to them, which makes them reluctant to do what you want.

The point is to support each other rather than blame each other, even when you're frustrated or don't understand why they're doing something. Find out what is behind their actions with an open mind, and find a compromise with them as opposed to telling them that they are failing at something.

One important thing to avoid is having the same disagreement over and over again. As disagreements come up, make a rule about it that both of you follow, rather than letting a disagreement fade without any resolution. But the key is that you both have to completely agree to the rule. Write it down separately if needed to refer back to so you don't end up in the same disagreement or with the same destructive behavior later on.

Action Plan for "Be Supportive" quality

Do things as a way to be helpful, caring and support them.

Let them express their feelings:

- ⊙ Let them verbally release their worries and problems.
- ⊙ Acknowledge and support their feelings.

Two-way conversations and support interests:

- ⊙ Talk about your day and what's going on in your life.
- ⊙ Let them talk without interrupting them.

Thoughtful acts:

- ⊙ Do household chores with a thought to how they like it.
- ⊙ Do specific things because they like it.

Take turns and compromise:

- ⊙ Take turns doing what each other wants.
- ⊙ Compromise to get both of your desires met.

Chapter 8

Team Quality #2

Be Uplifting

Positivity not Negativity

Kelly knew there were things that aggravated Brian in life. This wasn't a surprise. Things frustrated her too sometimes, but what she was drawn to, and found attractive, was when he had more of a positive vibe about him than a negative vibe.

To Kelly, life can be a series of aggravations or a series of happy things, depending on your mindset. Eventually, she communicated to him that she had an attraction to him more when he let the gloomy things go in life and embraced more of an uplifting presence overall.

Showing positivity instead of negativity is opting between two different ways of dealing with people, especially your spouse, and of looking at life in general. It's using a choice of words and behavior that is either bright and optimistic or tense and pessimistic. Even little, innocent comments can foster a negative atmosphere instead of a positive one, or can come across as complaining rather than a desire to be met.

Your spouse may be attracted to you when you comment on happy, upbeat things and what you're thankful for more often than resorting to grumbling about things you're aggravated about, sounding downbeat or expressing a doom and gloom attitude. It's easy to let things in life affect you and cloud how you express yourself. Constantly complaining about problems or ongoing issues with life may not be very attractive to your spouse.

Talk about what you want out of life as a positive thing more often than what you don't want out of life or what you want changed in life. For example, think about how often you talk about potential issues with the home itself. Striving for change is admirable and needed, but act from an uplifting stance rather than conveying the home has a series of problems to be fixed. Too much negativity can just be depressing to be around.

If your spouse, or someone else, says something positive or something they're happy about, don't offer a warning or a caveat to it. Let them enjoy their moment without trying to squash it a little bit. Again, choose to be optimistic with them, don't choose to be pessimistic to them. On the other side, if they say how a situation is difficult for them, don't compare it to how difficult another situation is for you.

What about when you dislike an action or behavior from your spouse? Flattery and rewarding the things you like from them works better for change than scolding or trying to punish behavior you don't like from them. Make them want to please you rather than simply trying to avoid your harshness. They will want to please you again in the future when you do this.

Brian has changed to reinforcing the positives rather than highlight the negatives to Kelly. Instead of harping on what he doesn't like, he says, "I love it when you do *this*, it really makes me want to do things for you." He realizes he will get better results with a positive vibe than a negative vibe.

Part of this entails changing from blaming them for their negative behavior to seeing what behavior of yours could be contributing to their actions. Or seeing that the way you're currently communicating with them may not be helping to improve the situation.

Sometimes saying something in a different way will get you the result you desire. Really think about how you can say something different from the way that has not given you what you're looking for. One way to do this is to think about it from how they're hearing something.

A lot of times it's not your expectation that's wrong, it's the way you deliver the message that could be different. For example, feeling like your hero, rather than a servant or being told what to do, could be the motivation they need. People don't like to be told what to do, but they do like to help others. Present it as a problem they can solve or can help you with.

Or find a benefit for them with your request. But make sure it's truly a benefit to them, not just what you see as a benefit. To do this, you have to see life from their eyes and what they want out of life, which is hard to do when you're only focused on what you want out of life at that moment.

Approach problems from the positive side, not the negative side. Instead of saying, "why do they do this frustrating thing I don't like", say "what can I do that would motivate them to do what I like instead". Be hopeful not cynical.

If you're trying to get them to change but doing it in a way that will hurt or insult them, it rarely has a good outcome. They likely won't suddenly change to become better, they will likely change something to hurt you like you hurt them. You want a win/win, not a lose/lose outcome.

If you want something from your spouse, ask for it without insulting them or acting frustrated. Use kind words and ask directly for what you want. For example, if the house is a mess, don't tell them they never clean up after themselves. Instead, ask if they could please clean up a certain area so it looks nice.

Be aware when you ask them to do something, that it doesn't come out as a harsh, demanding order like that of a manager/subordinate role. You may not be asking them in a nice, polite way, but rather in a way that sounds snotty. Have it come across as a choice they get to make to help you be happy.

When you say, "move your shoes please", it sounds like a demanding order to them, even though you're using the word please. However, when you say "when you get a moment would you mind moving your shoes so I don't trip over them", it sounds more like asking a request to them. This second way is much more likely to get the future results you're really looking for.

Another way to ask is to have your request come across as a favor to you because it's important to you, rather than telling them to do it or treating them like a child. Instead of telling them you want something done, let them know why it's so important to you, especially in an emotional sense. Otherwise they may not think it's that big of a deal or that you're just trying to run their life.

The key is to ask directly what you would like them to do, give them enough time to accomplish the project, don't hover around them to make sure it's done "correctly" and don't remind them to do it. If it hasn't been done after a certain amount of time, ask if they would have time to get to it soon. By asking them nicely a second time, instead of getting upset at them, they are much more likely to do it right away.

Warm, Pleasant, Cheerful

She never knew it was such a big deal to him. Just simply the act of Marie being cheerful, pleasant and smiling, in turn put a smile on Jeremy's face every time. She didn't realize the importance of her attitude toward him and others. Marie discovered that a warm disposition isn't being fake. It's choosing to be thoughtful about how her behavior affects him.

Maintaining a warm, pleasant and cheerful frame of mind can be very attractive to your spouse. Be a person that others want to be near because of your infectious perspective. A cheery attitude can be really uplifting to be around. Let people use your energy to make themselves feel better. Don't underestimate the power of simply smiling more often.

Have a mindset of wanting to uplift people and brighten their day a little. Be aware of how you greet people, especially your spouse. Be aware of how you interact with them. Your spouse may be impressed when you deal with others in a good-natured way, not criticizing or judgmental.

Kind words, kind thoughts, kind demeanor. Being genuinely kind to people can be appealing. Even if you're feeling agitated, don't let your emotions control an unkind reaction of being rude or inconsiderate. You can't control other people's behavior, but you do have control of your own.

It can be easy to act agitated or bothered, which includes a bad attitude even if your words are not bad. Your spouse doesn't want you to be fake, but they do want you to put frustrating thoughts out of your head so they're less likely to come out of your mouth, and to maintain a pleasant disposition without letting it fester inside of you.

You're a normal person and have negative emotions, but you can distinguish when to express them and when it's not necessary to. Even though these thoughts of annoyance are normal once in a while, realize that you do have the ability to stop yourself from overly expressing them.

Marie is careful not to over-think things, rush through good things in life or fixate on problems that might not even be there. When she slows down and just focuses on brighter aspects in life, the actual problems and their solutions can be much easier to find. She asks herself, "what can I do today to reduce someone's stress, not add to it, especially my spouse's?"

Being careful with your words is part of this, particularly toward your spouse. Making snarky, snide or snippy comments to your spouse are easy to let slip out, but can be extremely harmful to the relationship. Of all people, they are the one you should be most careful with your words. If it's even slightly unkind, it's the wrong thing to say.

Instead of saying something abrasive, derogatory or insulting, say something good about them or choose to stay silent. You may not agree with or understand everything they say or do, but try to lift them up or just go on with your life instead of knocking them down.

Your body language is part of this, such as eye rolling or hand gestures. Negative body language can be equally bad because they can convey a lot of unintended bad messages to them. They can feel you don't value their opinion, you feel superior to them or you think your thoughts are better than theirs.

Your tone of voice is part of this, such as using a frustrated, angry tone or indicating they should already know something. Even if you are trying to be nice, your tone of voice may give them the opposite impression. Along the same lines, be aware of non-verbal things you do, such as a heavy sigh.

Another key is to be careful about being unintentionally insensitive. Just in general, be careful being overly opinionated because you might insult or say something negative about something they like or feel proud of. You can make them feel bad without realizing it by overly expressing your opinions too strongly too often.

Think about how much you use teasing or sarcasm. It can go from playful to hurtful quickly. Putting someone down, even in a joking manner, can be very upsetting. You may think you're being funny, while they could take it as you're being unpleasant or unkind. A little may be fine with them, but just be aware not to overdo it.

Empathy, Encouragement, Appreciation

"You really did a fantastic job!" Richard had just completed a project at work and was telling Alice about it. She never held back in warming his heart with praise and compliments. He loved that about her! She was quick to show her appreciation for him or give him encouragement when he needed it most.

Be your spouse's biggest cheerleader in life. Make them feel like they are on top of the world and can do anything. Build them up and believe in them. They have enough people in this world who don't believe in them, including themselves at times, you are the one person who can really make a difference with this.

Being their biggest cheerleader is both being overt and obvious about lifting them up, and being very careful not to knock them down. It's seeing their side of things; it's what you say to them; it's showing how your life is better because they're in it. Three components help with this – showing empathy, encouragement and appreciation.

Empathy - they want some empathy from you for their situation and how they're affected by something. A hard thing to do, but usually needed, is to have empathy when you don't understand why they have a concern or a thought. Be careful moving forward with actions or words based on your feelings without stopping to think about their feelings regarding the matter.

There's a difference between being compassionate and showing empathy. Compassion can often be associated with bigger events and straight-forward emotions. Most people would have compassion for the death of someone's relative or a sudden job loss because they can understand the emotions and perspective of what that person is going through, and often offer to help.

But empathy is trying to see their side of an issue, especially when you don't completely understand their feelings about it or it's difficult to see their perspective and what they're going through. This is particularly hard to do when your own emotions are really high or nonexistent regarding a situation. You don't have to always do what they desire, but genuinely care about how they feel, take their issues seriously and adjust your behavior when appropriate.

You may have to focus more on empathy if you think about how something affects you, not how it affects them. You may be seeing everything through your eyes and your emotions, and have an automatic reaction to something that you don't agree with or don't understand. Don't just brush past their emotions about something, even if it seems silly to you.

It really helps to slow down and truly think about a situation from their side. How does something affect them, including your actions and behavior? What emotions are they going through? How difficult is a current situation for them?

Don't be dismissive of their thoughts, concerns or how they feel about something. Listen to them without invalidating what they say or minimizing their perception of it. When you don't understand something or it doesn't seem important, a gut reaction can be to dismiss it, not put any thought into it and refuse to change your behavior. When you do this, it can seem like you're not caring about them or their feelings at all.

A big part of empathy is not reacting defensively when they bring up an issue with you. Don't cloud the issue by bringing up their faults or saying they do the same thing as what they're upset about with you. If they tell you what they want, don't just ignore it or shift blame because you don't want to deal with it.

This is also true when you get irritated at their reaction to something you said or did. Don't get mad because their reaction irritates you without first thinking about how you were affecting them to begin with. Don't be more concerned with how they are treating you than with how their feelings were hurt in the first place.

A lot of this comes down to putting your feelings on hold for a minute when your spouse says something that you could immediately take issue with. It's okay at times to concede to their point, apologize and be understanding of their side of an issue. If you don't try to comprehend the situation they're in or their feelings, they will learn to not be open with you in the future.

One benefit to empathy is it allows you to stop and do some self-evaluation. It's easy to dismiss things someone says about you that you could work on for personal growth, but that doesn't mean those things aren't true. While you should believe in yourself, you also have to acknowledge that other people may see things in you that you are blind to.

Encouragement – be encouraging to them, especially when they need it most. If they seem happy or excited about something, be happy or excited with them. Or if they do something, give them praise for it. Sometimes it can be easy to inadvertently focus on yourself and forget about making them feel good.

Compliments can be a huge part of this. Tell them when you notice something attractive about them or how good they are at doing something. Some people don't get praised or complimented often in everyday life. So, they like it when you do this because they may not get that outside of the marriage.

It's very attractive when you show you value their thoughts about things. Ask their opinion on things and actually take their suggestions. Ask what they want instead of just going forward with what you want. For example, ask them what they would like for dinner or offer them a choice between two things.

Assume your spouse can do something rather than assuming they might screw it up. When you assume the negative, you can make them question their own skills and confidence which in turn can lead to them screwing it up. They can succeed or fail based in part on your encouragement and belief in them.

A way of insinuating a lack of trust in them is when you ask a question to make sure they did something. Unless it's obvious they didn't do something, trust them by not verifying it. Show them you believe they can handle the situation without your interference.

When Alice encourages Richard, it makes him happy and makes him want to do things for her more often. She gives him inspiration that he is capable of figuring out a problem for himself, but she is by his side against anything that comes at them in life. Similarly, Alice feels elated when Richard does the same.

Believe in your spouse even when they make mistakes and definitely don't berate them when they make one. Everyone is human and can make mistakes from time to time. Think twice before saying something that could hurt their feelings. It's better to not say something than to carelessly make them feel bad. Let them know you have confidence in them.

Another component of this is backing them up with other people. If they're in a disagreement with someone, don't take someone else's side against your spouse at that moment in front of them. This is especially true if it's a relatively small issue.

If it's a bigger or moral issue where you think your spouse is clearly in the wrong, you can gently talk to them about it in private. The main thing is to convey to your spouse that you are on their side in life, but maybe they can look at something a different way or from a different standpoint.

A key point of encouraging is to let go of resentment toward your spouse. It's easy to carry resentment of your spouse over things they've done in the past. That resentment can show up in your thoughts and actions toward them, but isn't productive for a healthy marriage.

Appreciation – telling them how proud you are of them can be extremely important. It doesn't have to be elaborate, even just a few words written or verbal can make them swoon. This is different than a compliment. It's showing them you appreciate who they are and what they do for others, especially you. Simple manners like saying please or thank you can be a simple way to show appreciation, but don't let it be the only way.

Verbalize what you're thinking. Tell them how much you appreciate what they do for the family or when they do nice things for you. Use examples of something they've done or said that reinforces your high opinion of what they do. Doing this in front of other people can also really make them feel good.

Make sure the comments are about them, not about you. For example, saying "I love you", "I miss you" or "I really like being with you" are good things to say. But ultimately they're about you and your feelings, not about giving appreciation for what they do. In addition to these things, also say "I love how hard you work for us" or "I really appreciate that you buy my favorite item at the store".

The look. Don't do this all the time and overdo it, but sometimes look at them with absolute adoration. Remind them through your eyes that you are still happy you both chose each other. Remind them through your eyes that you still think they are amazing and couldn't dream of being with anyone else.

Flexibly Enthusiastic

This wasn't his favorite thing to do. But you would never know it based on his attitude and actions. Walking was Kara's thing, not Cole's. But whenever she wanted to go for a walk, not only did he do it, he never showed a sign of reluctance. Cole knew that being flexible and enthusiastic about what Kara loved to do meant that she would return the favor when he wanted to do something that wasn't her thing. The key for Cole is that he didn't just do it, he did it with a great attitude.

Being flexible by having an open mind about things you normally don't do can be very attractive to your spouse. Things can go awry when you close yourself off from what they want to do and their desires, especially ones that are different than yours.

It simply means putting in effort for what is important to them and makes them happy. Putting in effort in the way that's most meaningful to them makes them feel like you really care. You may honestly care about them, but if you only do things that you enjoy doing without thinking about the things they enjoy, it can feel like you don't care as much as you really do.

This does not mean "sucking up" to your spouse and doing everything they want. It does not mean acting like a doormat just to please them. It does not mean changing who you are or suppressing yourself in any way.

There is a difference between expanding yourself to do something you normally wouldn't do and doing something that goes against your ethics. Being willing to explore things your spouse is interested in and experiment a little is important, especially if they're not asking you to go against your ethics for it.

Be more flexible by not getting caught up in what you want or like all the time. You can become too stubborn and unbending by being in that frame of mind. You don't want to bend over backwards to do it all, but there is a middle ground of being flexible for them more often and amenable to things that aren't your idea or when you would normally do them.

It's easy to automatically say "no" or knock down their ideas and suggestions. Be careful having that default response because you may come to realize fulfilling your spouse's request isn't that big of a deal after all and you might actually have fun with it. Try to say yes more than you say no.

Sometimes if you let your body go with the flow of doing an activity, your mind will catch up and get into it. That's not always the case, but it can happen more than you think. If you make your mind decide first, it's easy for your mind to just say no and not give the activity a chance to get enjoyable. Sometimes the mind must follow the body.

It's easy for you to get in a comfortable part of your life and want nothing to change from it. Remind yourself that to fulfill their requests, sometimes you do have to push yourself. Don't stop trying to identify or do the things that would make them happy.

Cole showing enthusiasm when he's doing these things is a big part of the excitement and enjoyment for Kara. If she feels he is just going through the motions or it's just an obligation he has to do, she doesn't receive enjoyment from it. He has a good attitude for her.

Your spouse wants to know that you aren't just accommodating them, but that you truly want to see them happy and fulfilled. When you don't react enthusiastically when fulfilling their desires, you can give the impression that you don't really care about what's important to them. It's essential to fulfill their needs enthusiastically because this is part of how you show that you care about them and what's important to them.

One of the best ways to be enthusiastic about their interests is for you to find a benefit for yourself of what they like and to take ownership of it in order to embrace what they enjoy. You can add something to their request or create emotions and feelings inside of you to control your response to it. When you feel you control part of it and take ownership of part of it, you will find it much easier to fulfill their needs and bring a better attitude toward it. You are doing this for yourself because you are finding a way to benefit from it, even though it's their request.

Take for example if they like to go to football games together. You don't have to like the football game itself, but you can find other benefits for yourself when fulfilling their need. If it's a little bit of a drive, you can spend the night in a hotel, get breakfast in your favorite out of town café and get to people watch if you enjoy that. Plus, you get to spend time with your spouse and talk while driving to the game.

Build Them Up to Others

It happened again. Only this time, Rachel didn't feel good about it. She had gone to lunch with her friend and it seemed like all they did was complain about little irritations in their marriages and with their husbands. Dennis is a good person and a good husband, but it just became a habit to vent about minor things to her friend.

She didn't feel good about it because she realized she was painting a really bad picture about him to her friend. And it didn't help the marriage because the things she complained about didn't actually bother her that much. It was just more of a way to bond with her friend over lunch, which wasn't okay.

It's okay to talk to other people about problems in your marriage. Especially if you feel in danger. It's important to feel safe in your marriage and to get good help for a marriage having problems. Absolutely do not ignore warning signs if there are serious problems or dangerous situations.

However, too often you may not really want advice about a marriage problem. You just want to vent about your spouse and have your friends agree with your point of view. The issue is that it's not helpful and it's definitely not uplifting your spouse. You are getting support in a way that doesn't help the marriage and ultimately doesn't really help you as an individual.

Getting advice on a problem in the marriage can be a good thing. Just make sure you are actually wanting legitimate advice and willing to listen, even if people tell you that you're the one in the wrong on a situation. Give a fair and accurate description of the situation without any derogatory comments about your spouse.

If you're trying to be uplifting to your spouse and be united with them, you can't portray them as being less than that to other people. You should be building them up in your eyes and in everyone else's too.

Everyone else should see the immense pride you have in both your spouse and for the marriage itself.

If you make snide remarks about them to your friends or family, it can be hard for you to not let these types of remarks slip out when you're around your spouse. It can become an unconscious habit because you're used to doing it when they're not around. So even if you're just joking or venting, be aware that talking down about your spouse to other people can be an issue.

The more you complain about something, the bigger it seems to be. It could be a small thing that doesn't really bother you that much, but turns into a big thing in your mind as you over-focus on it and as you get reinforcing feedback from your family and friends.

When you talk negatively about your spouse to others, three things can happen. First, you ignore their positive attributes as a spouse. Second, you stop trying to find a solution to the problem because you're in complaining mode instead. Third, you stop thinking about what actions of yours could be contributing to the problem and to their actions.

Venting to friends or family about relatively minor issues in your marriage can have a longer lasting effect than you think. That mentality often doesn't stop just with in that moment you're venting. It carries on after that. The more you talk about your spouse's faults, the more you view them as "bad". But, the more you talk about their positive traits, the more you view them as "good".

You and your friends may be bonding when you talk to each other about your problems. However, you may not realize how bad it may be to the marriage to bond in this manner or how hurt / embarrassed your spouse may be when you do it. You and your friends may understand not to take these "gripes" seriously, but your spouse may not understand this the same way.

You can still bond by talking about the marriages – just decide to do it in a way that is more productive in achieving a happy marriage. Uplift everyone's marriage by talking positive things about each marriage whenever possible.

Action Plan for "Be Uplifting" quality

Have a kind, positive energy about you and lift them up with a good-natured attitude.

Positivity not negativity:
- ⊙ Say positive things more often than gloomy things.
- ⊙ Ask nicely for things rather than a demanding order.

Warm, pleasant, cheerful:
- ⊙ Have a warm, joyful, kind attitude and smile often.
- ⊙ Limit snide words, irritated tone or bad body language.

Empathy, encouragement, appreciation:
- ⊙ Compliment and encourage, not dismissive of concerns.
- ⊙ Be their biggest cheerleader in life, even their mistakes.

Flexibly enthusiastic:
- ⊙ Be more flexible about things you normally don't do.
- ⊙ Show enthusiasm when doing things together

Build them up to others:
- ⊙ Don't talk negatively about them, unless in danger.
- ⊙ Be careful of comments that put them in a bad light.

Chapter 9

Team Quality #3

Be Easy Going

Let Some Things Slide

Dixon was about to say something. Hannah had left her coffee cup on the counter instead of putting it in the dishwasher. Yes, it was an irritation to him, but was it really that big of an issue in the larger scope of life? Dixon found that if he just let the little or minor irritations go without saying anything, he forgot about it in a manner of minutes.

But if he expressed every irritating thought that came into his mind, they could be unhappy with each other for days. He had to decipher the big things that should be addressed with Hannah from the little things that should stay unspoken. He got to choose whether their evening together would be a happy one or an unhappy one.

Distinguish between the big issues in life that really matter and the small issues that don't matter very much or will likely be forgotten quickly. If it's a big issue to you, your spouse would want you to address it directly. But if it's a small or minor issue, that's where they want you to have an easy going attitude to just let it go without saying anything.

If something really bothers you, talk to your spouse about it. They know that if you never disclose anything that bothers you, it will start to build frustration toward them. They do want an open dialogue, but leave out any snarky tone or attitude. You might be right in what you're saying, but how you say it is vital.

However, doing this all the time about everything in life can be frustrating to your spouse. In your mind, you may think that being transparent with your thoughts, emotions and what you're feeling is good for open communication. You may think that will bring a certain closeness to the relationship.

So you start being upfront about all your feelings, especially the ones bothering you. If something ruffles you, particularly with your spouse, you may be quick to point it out and make a comment about it. You may think you are being honest, communicating with them and just stating a fact about something.

Your spouse may not see it that way. They may see it as you being easily irritable or upset at too many things in life. Or that you aren't letting little things in life pass and focus on the overall larger aspects of life. While you mean to simply state a fact or opinion about something, they may hear it as a complaint or criticism and be put off that you're letting too many things get to you.

Realize that some minor things in life are not the end of the world and don't need to be verbalized. There are so many big things in life you should worry about and get frustrated with, you don't need to add to it with relatively minor stuff that doesn't significantly alter your well-being.

There are two common examples of this. Don't get irritated when they do or say something in a way that contrasts with how you would. Remember, getting irritated at how they go about life isn't fair to them. Second, don't get upset when you ask their opinion on something and you don't like the answer they gave. Remember, you're the one that asked them.

Along with this, your spouse may want you to not appear to be disagreeable. Don't nitpick things they do or say, especially if it's a minor thing. Don't often say the opposite or contradicting comments to what they say. Don't make counter arguments to a simple passing thought of theirs. Don't ask them a question, then critique or ignore their answer.

Don't nit-pick. Life is not perfect. If you try to make all the little things in it perfect, you're going to make yourself and people around you miserable. Be conscious that even your small comments or questions may sound innocent to you, but can sound to them like you're trying to find fault or over focus on minor aspects of life.

When you nit-pick little things, you can sound like you should have extra special treatment or that things must be perfect in order to be blessed with your presence. Instead, you want to communicate that you are so head over heels in love with your spouse that you just enjoy being with them without things being perfect.

Another thing that can be off-putting or unattractive to your spouse is automatically rebutting what they say with your own opinions, or even facts, a lot. You don't have to agree with them, but don't disagree either. Get out of the thinking that every tiny thing must be pointed out or rebutted.

Be careful with questioning them, correcting them or shooting down their ideas. If they say something or have a suggestion you don't fully agree with, determine if it really matters that much. If it doesn't matter, don't say anything and don't immediately try to make a counterpoint. Especially if it's a small, inconsequential thing.

Sometimes they want more of a laid-back exchange between you two, rather than lively banter or a competitive debate. Don't think everything has to be a topic of debate by offering a contradiction to what they do or to a simple comment they make. This includes asking questions. Ask questions to gather information, not to see if they did something right or if they did it the way you would.

You should have opinions and voice them. You're not suppressing yourself or playing dumb. Just acknowledge that not everything in life needs to be disputed, a clash of views or a gold star for being the one with the correct facts. Not every thought that is different from yours needs to be rebutted, especially if you sound a little sarcastic, slightly insulting or critical in nature.

It can be easy to think that you should be offended by something they say or do, when in reality it's just a minor passing thought of theirs. They know you have different thoughts than they do, but they don't want to feel bad for expressing their thoughts or doing certain actions. You don't have to mirror those things. Just realize they may want you to let certain things slide without over-reacting, getting offended or upset about it.

Your spouse doesn't want you to be silent about what's important to you or to only mimic their thoughts. They're not trying to hold you down in any way. They admire your intelligence and want it to be on display in the marriage.

However, they don't want you to constantly contradict, critique, second guess them or offer your own opinion if the issue isn't really that big of a deal. Determine if it's a minor thing that doesn't matter in the long run, or if it's a serious matter that really does need a calm discussion around it.

Give Them the Benefit of the Doubt

"Did Nathan do this on purpose?" Monica thought to herself. He knows the kind of chicken she likes from the store. This wasn't it. She came close to blowing up about it to him. Instead, she asked, "Is there a reason you got this chicken instead of my usual?" The response back was, "Yes, they were out of your usual, so I thought you would like this one instead."

Now she felt terrible. She was about to explode like a volcano when he was just trying to do something nice for her. Disaster averted because she chose to give him the benefit of the doubt and did not assume he did it on purpose to be uncaring.

Your spouse wants you to give them the benefit of the doubt to assume their intentions are good and not trying to hurt you or be thoughtless toward you. You may have an immediate reaction to something they did or said, only to find out later that's not the message they meant to convey at all.

You get to decide what you get in return from them with your own actions. You can either over analyze things they say and do, which can result in them limiting their interaction with you in the future. Or you can give them the benefit of the doubt that they don't mean harm to you, which will encourage them to continue being open with you in the future.

Don't look for "gotcha" moments with your spouse, where you're trying to spot offenses before they really pop up or before you know all the facts. No one wants to feel like they're being watched for times when they might be screwing up and made to feel bad. You should be ready to overlook things that could be misconstrued, rather than calling your spouse out for ways they could be messing up.

A lot of this comes down to simply how you view situations. If you look for bad intentions, you can find them. If you look for good intentions, you can find them. The situation is the same, but your perspective is what is different. It can be unattractive and unfair to them when you perceive slights that aren't actually there at all, except in your mind.

Part of the reason frustration may grow in you is because you may think they are trying to take something from you and to be selfish. Try to change this thought process into thinking that they are simply trying to be happy while also keeping you happy. They usually are not doing anything on purpose to hurt you.

In addition, know the difference between them having truly bad, destructive behavior and you being slightly uncomfortable because they're having an off moment or day. Look at their track record and history to think about if their behavior is out of ordinary for them. Was this a rare occurrence that should be overlooked and not mentioned? Or is it a regular pattern that should be addressed?

To go along with this, remember there's a difference between them being slightly insensitive and them being deliberately hurtful. If it's not intentionally malicious, sometimes you have to just let some things go and not get upset because not everything will be said and done exactly the way you think it should be. Be offended by truly malicious things, not by every little thing people do and say.

Monica doesn't draw her own conclusions about what Nathan's thinking, feeling or going to do. When she tries to anticipate these things, she tends to get disappointed before he even has a chance to do anything. She can fall into the trap of seeing malicious acts and intentions from him that simply weren't there to begin with.

You may have to tell your emotions to take a seat for a minute, especially when your spouse is letting their own emotions out. Maybe you need to give someone or something a second chance instead of making a snap decision. Maybe you need to stop to think about why they did something, other than just trying to upset you.

Everyone gets irritated or grumpy when they get denied something that's important to them. It may not be the best response to have, but it's human. Look past this outward emotion of theirs and work on how you can help the situation and the marriage, rather than just getting mad at their emotion about it.

This is a really important point. It's not always easy to give them the benefit of the doubt, but instead to default to calling them childish, immature or that they are showing entitlement about something. But really it could just be that they're hurt over being denied something important to them.

Before you react to something they said or did that irritates you, even if your irritation is warranted, pause to think about why. If they're not being denied something important to them, they could be hungry, tired or stressed. Or you don't know the whole story about why they did or said something and you need more clarity.

When they try to do something nice for you, don't focus on one little aspect that wasn't quite right. Look at the whole picture of what they're trying to do. They're trying to do something good, but all aspects of it won't always be exactly the way you want it to be.

Another way to give benefit of the doubt is when you are telling them something. Be clear and direct, but be careful over explaining things based on previous discussions or prior situations you've been in. You may be talking down to them based on your own past history, without even realizing it.

Limit Advice, Rigidness and Leading

Carly didn't mean to do it. She was just trying to be helpful with her suggestion. Instead, Leon took it as her not viewing him as a capable adult and trusting his decision-making abilities. She had to remind herself the way he was cooking was different than the way she would do it, but it wasn't necessarily incorrect or wrong. It was just simply the way he liked to do it.

This was just one of a dozen minor differences between the way they each did things. She was determined to let him be different than her, so her new motto became "different doesn't mean wrong." Her suggestions, even though well-intended, weren't always the right things to say.

Your spouse may want you to go with the flow more, instead of often running the show. Take a step back and let them decide what's best at times. Trying to direct things all the time doesn't work, which can come out in 3 ways – giving too much unsolicited advice, being too rigid about your way and leading too often.

It can wear them down to continually hear you try to run, control or direct things in life often. Sometimes they want you to trust them when they are doing something or when they say they have something handled, and not try to intervene. When they do something you disagree with, ask yourself a question. Is it diminishing you or others; affecting your attraction to them; or just different than how you would do it?

It can be easy to think it's your responsibility to "right the wrongs" in life. Not just your life, but other people's, especially your spouse. While that's admirable to make the world a better place, you can often over-step and veer into being controlling rather than helpful. Step back to see it's not always your role to determine how things are done.

Limit advice. You may think you're trying to be helpful when you make suggestions or give advice. Your spouse may take it as judgmental, condescending or dictating. Sometimes you need to let them run their own life, even if it's different than how you would do it. It can be easy to sound like you're trying to direct their life, along with your own, because you're just trying to be helpful with suggestions.

Instead of being helpful, you can sound controlling or bossy to them. Your way may be right for you, but it's not necessarily right for them. Give them room to do things in their own unique way that isn't detrimental to you or the marriage. Sometimes they aren't looking for, or appreciate, the help you want to give them. Instead, it can be frustrating to them.

Practicing patience is the key. When they do something you wouldn't do, take a breath, practice patience and stay quiet. Don't cross the line from trying to be helpful and concerned about them to treating them like a child instead of as an adult who is allowed to make their own decisions, and capable of it.

Sometimes they may want to make a simple statement about something without having you question it, critique it or try to offer some type of alternative regarding it. Even if you think it's an important viewpoint to talk about, waiting until a later time to bring it up might be more appropriate. Let them take the conversation where they want it to go rather than where you want it to go or to scrutinize them.

It's okay to be a caring, nurturing person, but don't overdo it. Back off from questioning them, telling them what they should do or trying to overly control situations around you. Ask yourself, "does this thing they do differently really affect me directly? Is it really affecting my life?" If the answer is no, then don't mention it to them. They have a right to do things differently or to have a different agenda than you.

You can fall into this trap when you try to disguise giving advice as simply stating your opinion without someone asking for it. People should be able to have their own opinions without having you trying to persuade them into your way of thinking. You can be viewed as over-stepping when you do this.

Note that there is a difference between giving unwarranted advice and guarding against something bad happening. For instance, telling your spouse how to drive to a destination they clearly know how to get to is unwarranted advice that should be avoided. But if they drive past a freeway exit you know they need to take, let them know that they just went past their exit, but not in a reprimanding, disapproving way.

Limit rigidness. Be bendable, not rigid in life. Be careful about being too rigid or too structured with things in life. Allow the plans inside your head to be moldable. When you do something, think about how your actions will affect others around you. Let your spouse's plans take precedence at times, even when it's in opposition to yours. Definitely don't have a meltdown or irritation over it.

When you're too particular about how things are done or doing only what you want to do, you don't leave your mind open to a different way of doing something or to find a compromise. When you're rigid about wanting things to be your way, you can sound demanding or controlling. Instead, they may want you to be more adaptable and to slow down. Don't get so focused on what you want that you forget to see if you're being unreasonable.

One of the major missteps you may make is expecting your spouse to do little things the way you do them, so be receptive to different ways. It's easy to fall into the trap of trying to turn your spouse into a mini version of yourself, or worse, acting like a parent to your spouse telling them what to do.

It's okay to have some preferences in life, but be careful being overly specific about things or having too many things that you're too specific about. Having a checklist for your life, and especially for other people, can backfire because life rarely goes smoothly if you don't allow some flexibility to it. This is especially important if your spouse doesn't like to rock the boat because you can easily appear to be dictating.

Even if you like doing things for people, you can still be rigid if you only do what you want to do for them and when you want to do it. You may consider yourself a generous person, but if you aren't bending a little bit to incorporate what they want and when they want it, you could be considered too rigid in your actions.

Sometimes Carly has to go at Leon's pace. If Leon says he will do the dishes, he may want to wait until after he does something else first, rather than in the timeframe she thinks it should be done in. She also tends to make decisions or talk about issues quicker than he does, so she needs to give leeway to go at his speed at times.

Limit leading. Follow rather than lead sometimes. Sit back and let them decide what to do at times, rather than always stepping up to lead the way or suggest what to do. Ask them what they want rather than telling them what you want. Likewise, be aware if you're interrupting or dominating a conversation too much.

Don't tell them what to do, be demanding, dictate how things should be or insinuate that what they're doing is wrong. You can give the appearance that you are trying to steamroll them, especially if you have a take charge personality. Trust them to solve issues themselves, even if it's different than how you do it.

If you see an issue, come to them with the problem and an opinion of what could be done, if you have one. But don't tell them what has to be done or already have your mind made up of what should be done. Ask them what they think of the situation and give credence to their ideas and suggestions.

Be careful about taking over projects you're working on together or jumping in to help them on something they're doing themselves. It can be easy to jump in and help them, but sometimes they just want to do it themselves without any assistance, input or comments from you. You can ask if they would like some help, but don't just jump in.

Don't make big decisions without talking to them first. You're a team, so you have to consult each other and make decisions together. Collaborate rather than acting solo. Collaboration means you're not just running with what you feel is best. Make it feel like you both share control of the decision to be made.

Handle Frustration Well

They were both guilty of it. They both knew this was a bad trait, even before they got married. Blake knew he needed to control his emotional temper when something in life frustrated him. Cassandra knew she had to control her emotional outbursts when they disagreed on something and not get defensive when he shared his true feelings about something.

It felt silly at first, but they started closing their eyes and counting to 10 when either of them felt anger or an overly emotional reaction coming on. But it usually worked. When it didn't work to calm them down, they would go take a walk around the block to think about something other than the frustration or over-reaction they were feeling at the moment.

Most people agree that acting out in a physical way when you're frustrated is not okay. But remember that acting out in a verbal way when you're frustrated can also be bad and very unattractive behavior. Both ways can be destructive in a relationship.

Disagreements happen in marriage. It's how you handle those disagreements that make a strong marriage. Let them state their true feelings without getting defensive or upset. You can't verbally explode, lash out insultingly or fall apart emotionally when something doesn't go your way or they say something you don't like. Accept that you won't always agree on everything.

Have a calm, rational discussion and amiably disagree if it comes to that. This is having control over your emotions and the words you use. Think about how something will come across to them. Find a way to say it in a nice way without snapping at them. Even if you feel justified, it's not okay to say hurtful things.

Say something constructive instead of just a biting remark or losing control of your emotions. If you need to take a break from communicating before you let your frustration boil over and you say something you will regret, let them know that. It's okay to take a breather to calm down a little bit and come back to the issue at another time.

When you're upset and you want to state how you're feeling in that moment, be careful not to make it sound like that's how you feel overall about them. When you make a sweeping statement, it can be hard for them to determine that's only how you feel right now and not completely about them, which can be very hurtful to them.

When you and your spouse get into a discussion, disagreement or a difference of opinion, don't fall into a bad habit of focusing on winning or trying to be right. Don't treat it like head-to-head competition in which you don't listen to the reason they want something, what their feelings are about it or what alternative benefit would be okay for them.

You can appear combative and argumentative when you dismiss any thought that goes against what you're saying, even if there's some truth to it. Don't get so stuck on your stance that you can't admit that what they're saying has some validity to it. There is often a little bit of validity on both sides of a discussion, but you have to be willing to let yourself see it.

Don't get focused on being right and making sure they see that they are wrong or try to force an apology. When you get caught up in who's right and who's wrong, it rarely has a good outcome. It stops all momentum of having a good conversation. Don't ignore and deflect everything they are saying and come at them with something to prove.

Be careful with trying to prove that you are strong and won't be walked all over. Step back and realize that giving something to them doesn't make you weak or wrong. It's simply stating that you put a high value on their happiness, knowing that they in turn will do the same thing for you.

This is a key point for harmony in the marriage - be okay with not always getting your way or doing what you feel is best some of the time. When in a disagreement, accept that sometimes you will get your way and sometimes they will get their way. Their needs, wants or desires are as legitimate as yours.

Sometimes Blake has to trust Cassandra when they disagree on a decision to be made. Sometimes Cassandra has to do the same and trust Blake's decision. They may still be uncomfortable about it, but they show trust in each other and they don't throw a fit about it.

Frustration happens in life. Your spouse may want a peaceful environment by having problems, issues or drama be toned down and dealt with in a more subdued manner. You don't have to ignore problems, just don't over-react to them or make them worse with your reactions. Find different ways to deal with things and stay calm.

Don't sulk, whine or have an angry outburst when you are upset. You can calmly talk about it, but be careful sounding bitter about your frustration. Or just pour your enthusiasm and energy elsewhere and remain in a good mood. Your spouse will be attracted to this behavior rather than acting immature.

While it's expected to get frustrated with life at times, you need to be able to control that frustration. Don't verbally snap at people. Make sure to cool down before talking if you need to. This can help to avoid angry outbursts or saying something in the heat of the moment that you will regret.

Remain under control and maintain your presence about you. Don't back down from conflict, but know how to express yourself to keep your anger and temper in check so it doesn't explode. Don't yell, get angry, lose your temper or your patience. There usually is no justification for outrageous behavior no matter what the situation is or what another person does.

It's important to take time for yourself. One of the reasons you can get into a frustrated mindset and release it outwardly may be because you don't make time in your day just for yourself. Even if it's only for a few minutes, do things that make you relax and let go of some of the tension from life.

You can do different things to accomplish this. Spend time doing a hobby, spend time alone, do a physical activity or get together with friends. This type of self-care can be helpful and important to being able to help keep yourself more calm and relaxed.

Some kind of physical activity can be a great stress reliever. It releases endorphins to help keep your mood upbeat and happy. It is a great way to engage with people, whether it be your spouse or friends. Even something as simple as a 15-minute walk around the block can be calming.

Stress and anxiety can be increased when you don't get a proper amount of sleep each night. Talk with your doctor or do some research to determine how much sleep is right for you. You can also take a few minutes each day to just sit, close your eyes and relax. Try to put everything out of your mind for those few minutes, without too much background noise to distract you.

Another way to reduce stress is to talk to someone other than your spouse from time to time about what's frustrating or on your mind. It can be easy to unload constantly to your spouse, which isn't fair to them. It's okay to talk to them occasionally about these things, but also read self-help books or talk to a friend on occasion. Don't make your spouse your only outlet for frustrations in life.

If you still feel you need additional help, talking to a therapist or counselor can be invaluable. It can help to talk to someone without any pressure and that you don't have an emotional attachment to. Sometimes just being able to talk to someone without worrying about how it affects them is what really helps you.

Action Plan for "Be Easy Going" quality

Be easy going and relaxed in life, especially towards them.

Let some things slide:

- ⊙ Let small issues go without nitpicking.
- ⊙ Don't contradict their thoughts often.

Give them the benefit of the doubt:

- ⊙ Give benefit of the doubt that their intentions are good.
- ⊙ Step back from over-analyzing what they do, say or mean.

Limit advice, rigidness and leading:

- ⊙ Back off from trying to run, control or direct things often.
- ⊙ Trust them to solve issues themselves without intervening.

Handle frustration well:

- ⊙ Control your temper when something in life frustrates you.
- ⊙ Don't focus on winning/being right when you disagree.

Chapter 10

Team Quality #4

Be Enticing

Visual Connection Using a Team Approach

Ethan had been wrong. He thought it wasn't that important to Melanie. He knew he let his wardrobe and grooming habits slip, and was not at a healthy weight according to his doctor. It wasn't the only one, but his appearance and health was one factor in the emotional connection she felt with him, partly because he takes her preferences into consideration rather than just ignoring it.

He had two choices. He could get mad at her for how innately felt and make her feel bad for her feelings and emotions around it. Or he could have empathy for it and make it a team effort, knowing that everyone feels a closeness to another person in their own way and one way is not superior to another.

Our desires and preferences are part of what attracts us to our spouse. Your spouse may have a desire for kind words and romantic gestures. But they may also have a preference for certain things they can visually see. The bond they feel with you through their eyes may have a bigger impact than you realize, equal to those other things.

Your spouse's desire is not just for the visual thing that they're wanting, it's for the connection to you that they feel with the fulfillment of it. It is partially a preference they have, but it's also truly one of the emotional connection points for them. This is similar to whatever makes a point of connection for you, such as having an intimate conversation.

You own your body and get to control how you look. But it is also good to have empathy for what they have a partiality to. Don't make them feel bad for having visual preferences or for the closeness they gain from it. As long as they're being respectful and not saying anything offensive, let them be honest about what they innately most like.

It's your ability to approach a sensitive topic like this with empathy, a team effort to work together and an openness to view their preferences as something worth doing that can be attractive to them. Support each other to show their desires are as valid as yours. For the visual part, it's a mixture of listening to them, fulfilling it as best you can to keep a close connection, and yet still feeling like you have control over your own body.

This can include four main areas: 1) grooming and hairstyle; 2) clothing; 3) physical self, which includes making healthy choices, having a little muscle tone and simply seeing you naked more often; 4) balancing appeal vs. appropriate.

Grooming and hairstyle - your spouse can be attracted to you when you have certain personal grooming habits that appeal to them. This can include good posture, personal hygiene and how you smell wearing perfume or cologne.

Wearing certain hairstyles that they most like may be important to them. You can have a casual hairstyle, but still in a way that they have a preference for. It might take some time and effort, but remember that it also takes time and effort for them to meet your important desires too.

Clothing - think about, and listen to, what your spouse finds appealing regarding clothing. It's easy to get caught up in what you normally wear without stopping to consider what you could do differently for them. Pay attention to aspects of your clothing style and what your spouse finds desirable, within reason.

Be a little flexible and accommodating with what you wear based on some of their preferences and the connection they can get from it. What you wear can definitely have an impact on this. Have clothes that fit well and your spouse enjoys seeing on you. Ask your spouse what they most like in certain situations.

Getting clothes as a present may be a clue of what they would like to see on you. Yes, the gift might be more for them, but what they do for you when they see you wearing it can be a gift to you. They are trying to tell you what they like and as a result, it would put them in a mood to do what you would like and appreciate.

Don't fall into an automatic routine with your clothes. Put some thought into it based on what you know they enjoy seeing. Pay attention to what you're wearing in certain situations and what they've commented on in the past. This may mean dressing up a little more when going out with them, or maybe a slightly different style than you automatically would pick.

Your spouse may want to see different sides of you in regard to appearance. At various times, they want to see sides of you that's casual, fun, sporty, sexy or elegant. They know you have many different facets to your personality, so they want to see those different facets in your appearance too. Don't get stuck wearing the same type of outfit all the time.

Physical self — work together and support each other to enjoy having an active way of life and healthy habits. You don't have to look like, eat like or work out like a fitness model, but your spouse might want each of you to make the right choices for being health conscious. Don't forget how important eating well, exercise and having a little bit of muscle can be for you overall.

Valuing a healthy lifestyle and a team effort to do the right things to achieve it could be what they're looking for. While anyone judging you, including your spouse or yourself, is never acceptable, there is a difference between that and them being respectful about what appeals to them as a way of living.

Your spouse probably likes some of the things you dislike about your own body and definitely doesn't want a perfect body from you. In a lot of instances, you can be a harsher critic of your appearance than they are. They likely see you in a much better way than you may think and generally don't see perceived flaws that you may see in yourself.

A desire your spouse may have is to see you naked more often. It's understandable that some people have some anxiety with being naked, even in front of their spouse. However, when you hold yourself back from showing your body to them because of insecurity reasons, they can feel like you are holding back because of them.

This is the same way you may feel when they hold themselves back from you emotionally and verbally. Be brave to find a way past these types of insecurity issues you may have so you can both be open with each other and trusting of each other.

Balancing appeal vs. appropriate - be willing to be visually appealing for your spouse, even in ways you normally wouldn't do, but within reason and without going too far. Again, find the right balance between your control of your body and empathy for what they find appealing.

At the same time, make sure you adhere to your values and morals. For example, it's important to listen to your spouse about what clothing style they find attractive, but if it violates your code of being appropriate, don't feel obligated to do it. Empathy doesn't mean you have to blindly do what they ask.

Ethan lets Melanie feel safe to open up about what she finds visually appealing on him, without making her feel bad, and while still keeping in mind his own ethical code of conduct. He doesn't make her feel bad about what she desires, but he balances it with what he feels is appropriate too.

Sometimes that balancing act can be hard. Don't get stuck in the mode of thinking that since something doesn't affect your own marital bond when denied, then it shouldn't affect them so heavily. When they're chastised for what they find visually appealing, they feel their emotions and feelings are being disregarded. You know how you feel when they disregard your feelings and emotions over something that's important to you.

Don't Put More Effort For Others Than Your Spouse

She didn't even think about it, but it was the same thing every night and most weekends. Cathy got up in the morning and inspected herself before she went to work. Her hair was done well, her clothes looked brilliant, her make-up was just right. She was set to go to work. Upon returning home, it was the complete opposite. Her look completely changed.

Terrence expected her to be comfortable at home after a long day at work, but he wished there would be a balance between comfort and still trying to have a look that he would appreciate since she tries to have a look that her workmates appreciate.

She knew he was right. She put a lot of effort into her appearance at work and less effort when she was at home. It doesn't have to be the same style of clothes, hair and grooming, but there should at least be similar value between how she looks at home for her spouse and outside of it.

Your actions may inadvertently indicate that you value how you look for other people more than how you look for your spouse. Think about the clothes and hairstyle you wear at home and after work. Realize if you're dressing nice during the day at work and changing into clothes and hairstyle at night and on the weekends that's comfortable but a look that they don't prefer.

You can still be comfortable at night but find comfortable clothes and hairstyle that are also preferential to your spouse. They may notice what you wear and like certain things more than others. Show they mean enough to you to do what they have a partiality to.

You don't have to take hours getting ready or spend an excessive amount of money. They just want to see that you are putting in some effort everyday into what is important to them, rather than just doing it for special events. There is a balance between very little effort and doing way too much.

Terrence and Cathy thought back to their early days together. Back then, even after a long day at work, they still tried to visually impress each other. After a while, it was easy to get in the habit of only being comfortable around each other and not think about how they look to the other one as much.

There is no strict measure of what each person should look like. The needs of people are individualized for each person, so you only need to listen to yourself and to your spouse on this issue and think about what they find most desirable, not what other people think you should look like.

Flirty and Seductive

"It's important to me that I feel sensually wanted and have the anticipation of what's coming next," she said to him. Marco showed his cute, wholesome side often and Tara loved that about him. But sometimes she also wanted him to show his sexy, sultry side. She needed that feeling inside of her that he finds her desirous, while letting the arousal build up. Actually, they both wanted to see that side in each other more often.

Flirting is one way to show your interest in your spouse, attract them and get their attention. Flirtation can help your spouse feel amorous and that you're enamored with them. You do this by using flirty, charming words; innocent yet suggestive touching; provocative, sexy actions.

Being seductive and flirtatious is bridging that gap between normal everyday interactions and giving them a hinting anticipation of what's to come later on. You are being tempting or charming and making them feel pursued or that you're in the mood to be pursued by them.

Show them you can switch back and forth between being cute / wholesome and being sexy / vivacious. Show your sensuality and how you find them desirous. It's done with words and body gestures, rather than being demanding, bratty or juvenile for their attention, or showing your virtuous side all of the time.

When it comes to flirtatious words, start small then continue to escalate and build. Make a point to make them smile and feel sensual. Flirty words don't have to be direct to start out and it doesn't have to be an obvious sexual comment.

Compliments can be a beginning form of flirting and are about making them feel good. The easiest thing you can do is to compliment something they're wearing, such as clothing or jewelry. Some people take a lot of pride in their fashion sense and what they put on, so they may be pleased with your thoughts.

More advanced flirtation takes it a step further and is about making them feel desired. For example, tell them they look sexy in their clothes rather than they just look nice. Tell them you can't wait to taste their lips when you get home rather than just that you're thinking about them.

There are many ways to talk about or write out these kinds of things. Remind them of a past experience together; let them know how much they excite you; tell them what you would enjoy doing to them; tell them what they can do that you would like.

Marco brushed up against Tara and said, "I had such a good dream about you the other night, but the details would make you blush." If Tara wants to continue this flirtatious vibe, she will signal to him for more explicit details. If she doesn't do this, he simply waits until a time she's more receptive to it.

Your spouse may want touch as a way to show your enticing interest in them. Start out the day or night with innocent little physical touches. Nothing overtly sexual at first, but enough to show your interest and to see how receptive they are at that moment. You're being suggestive and putting a feeler out there to see if they're receptive to be flirted with at that moment.

As you escalate, you can be more seductive and direct with it. Lightly tap or caress their butt. Lean in close to their neck and tell them they smell good as your fingers touch their body. Give them a sensual, passionate kiss or touch them more directly.

Sexy actions can take it a step further. You can look at them seductively or let them get an "accidental" peak at you. Let them see what you're wearing under your clothes, or not wearing. Dress provocatively when it's appropriate. You can leave sexy notes for them or leave them a trail of clothing to the bedroom.

When out somewhere with them, let them catch you staring at them. Admire them and show obvious appreciation for what you see. Especially do this when other people are around and show that everyone else pales in comparison to them.

A key thing to remember though is to take everything slow. Make interactions a little steamier and direct as you go along during the day. Keep aware of how they're reacting to make sure they're ready for that next level. Once they're comfortable with the little innuendos, you can move on to the more direct things.

Your spouse may want more direct, overt ways of showing your seductive and provocative side. This may feel uncomfortable. It may help you to just pretend to be an alter-ego for a while. This is a different person invading your body for a short time, and then returning to your normal self. After all, you can't feel guilty if it wasn't really you that was doing or saying something.

Bond Through Sexual Connection

They both felt it. The undeniable connection of skin to skin contact. Parker and Rowan knew it was only one of several different types of connection they felt for each other, but this one was equally important as the others. They both enjoyed the closeness they felt from this aspect of the relationship.

But the biggest key was that it was a balance of mutual pleasure between Parker and Rowan. Neither one felt like it was something they had to give to the other. Having a good, robust sex life is important to both of them. They both wanted that closeness they received from sexual contact.

There are lots of reasons people have sex, but two big reasons are for connection fulfillment and for tension release. For some people, frequent sexual contact is vital to them. They can feel better about the marriage when it's fulfilled. This is as much an emotional need as it is a physical need for them.

The connection fulfillment is when they feel emotionally connected to you through sexual contact. They may not even be overly physically aroused, but they have a longing to re-establish a connection with you in a way they can't do another way as easily. It can make them feel desired, wanted and important to you.

This is similar to the way some people get emotional intimacy through talking and opening up about their feelings. But instead, some people get this type of closeness through sex. It's the same type of bonding, but achieved through different means.

The tension release is when they put life on pause for a moment through sexual contact. The physical sensations and pleasure can be a way to unwind the stress of the day or week. It acts as a release valve to escape all the pressures they feel in life.

This is similar to the way some people use other types of activities to re-center themselves, ease tension and release stress in their body and life. They do it through exercise, reading, taking a bath, or even shopping. Others do it with sex.

When you understand what they truly get from sex, it can be easier to accept their initiations. Your spouse can be deeply hurt when this quality is absent or rejected. Remember that you both can feel pain and loneliness, but from different things in life.

Unless otherwise agreed, both spouses should be initiating sex some of the time. Making the effort to initiate can make them feel wanted and desired, and can be seen as an act of love. However, note that both spouses still reserve the right to decline sexual contact any time.

There are many areas of sexuality you can enjoy with your spouse, but here are three basic components to focus on in a sexual relationship.

Component 1 - Have sexual variety. Show genuine desire for sex itself and being adventurous in the bedroom. Be willing to try new things in order to stay out of a pattern or boring routine. Express and explore each other's desires for a change of pace variety. Being open and accepting of fulfilling each other's desires and turn-ons is the cornerstone of a satisfying sex life.

It starts with a positive mindset. Embrace sexuality, be open about it and don't view it as a taboo thing. Embrace your own arousals and your spouse's arousals. The arousals may be different from each other's, but if you both have an open mind about them and accept them, it can be a win/win for both of you.

Take turns to do one person's choice of sexual activity one night, then do the other person's choice of sexual activity the next time. There should be limits where you can say no, such as moral issues or doing truly uncomfortable things, but it should be more than just "that's not my favorite activity to do".

Taking turns to do what each of you enjoys most can be a key part of keeping intimacy alive in the bedroom. Sexual preferences can be very different and it's important that you both get what you want out of your mutual sex life. It's essential that both of you be enthusiastic when it's the other spouse's turn of choosing what to do.

As you do this and experiment, keep in mind one thing. Don't expect perfection the first couple of times you do something new. Most things take time to figure out exactly what you want, how to do it and get comfortable with it. Don't rush it or get frustrated when it's not what you pictured in your head right out of the gate.

Find a way to separate your "inside the bedroom" persona from your "outside the bedroom" persona. They can see, enjoy and distinguish the multiple sides of you. They see your parent side with the kids, your intelligent side, your kind side outside the bedroom and your wilder seductive side inside the bedroom.

One side of you does not diminish all the other sides in their eyes. Your spouse knows there's a difference between being one way in the bedroom and something completely different outside of it. They can appreciate and value this contrast, so don't be afraid to let go of your inhibitions and insecurities.

Component 2 - Pursue your sexual pleasure. Show genuine desire for your own pleasure. Be uninhibited and unashamed of pursuing what turns you on and what you enjoy sexually, providing you're not violating their consent. Leave out all subtly and outwardly show a desire for sex and for your own pleasure, without any embarrassment.

It doesn't mean you're an insatiable sexual being all the time or that's what defines you as a person. It means that you're insatiable in this given moment. At this moment, your sexuality is top of mind and what matters right now. The mental pleasure of seeing and hearing you enjoy sex can be intoxicating to your spouse. One of their biggest turn-ons may simply be seeing you turned on.

Don't let fear, anxiety, shame or guilt stop you from the fulfilling sex life you want to have and from letting them know what your fantasies, desires and turn-ons are. It's easy to let family, friends or others tell you what is right, wrong, normal or abnormal in the bedroom. But you should only listen to yourself, not everyone else. You have a right to your own desires.

Really figure out what areas of sexuality, and even specific sexual acts, arouse you and get your libido going by doing research if necessary. Figure out what your specific arousals are and communicate them to your spouse. Be clear to your spouse what turns you on and is important to you. Look into how nutrition, vitamins and various prescriptions, including birth control, can affect your libido.

When you communicate this, emphasize what they're doing that you want more of rather than what you want less of. People generally react better to what they're doing right than what they're doing wrong or even what they could do better, especially in the bedroom, including both your words and your actions.

Guide them to what feels good to you, without insinuating/acting like you're teaching them. Go over the top with encouragement and praise when they get close to what you like. Or tell them how much you liked it when they previously did something you liked. It's about positive encouragement, not conveying that they are missing the mark on something.

For example, instead of saying "don't do x, do y instead", only say "I really love y and would like more of it." If they don't do it how you would like, instead of saying "not like that, like this", only say "when you did it like this, it felt amazing!" You're emphasizing their actions that are good, not bad.

However, it's okay to communicate what you don't want to do because it is hard for you physically, mentally or emotionally. These are things that really are over the line of what you feel comfortable doing, not things that are simply not your preference to do, which you should take turns doing if it's something they enjoy and their preference.

Component 3 - Pursue their sexual pleasure. Show genuine desire for them and for giving them pleasure. Doing acts that focus on their pleasure as one part of an overall sexual event shows that you are putting their happiness as something worth pursuing. Make them feel really wanted with full effort, not just going through the motions.

Be a sexual ego booster for them. Let them know, through words, sounds and actions, what your desire for them is. Compliment them, tell them how much you want them and make them feel like a truly sexy person. Make sure they know, even if it's just through moans, how amazing they are and how much you're enjoying this sexual experience.

Be an active participant by actively enjoying their body with your eyes, hands, mouth and your whole body. Even if you have a libido that likes to follow their lead during sex, it doesn't mean you have to be passive about it. It may just boil down to showing a little more excitement and enthusiasm during sex. There's a difference between being receptive and being enthusiastically receptive.

They may also like you to actively enjoy your own body, which can be equally arousing to them. Not being afraid to touch yourself can be very stimulating to the sexual experience. Not only do they want to see and hear your pleasure, they may like the visual of this as well.

Be willing to change what you're doing and adjust to make sure they are enjoying the sexual experience as much as you. Don't ignore what they want to do and watch their body language to see if they seem to be moving a certain way or might be a little physically uncomfortable. It's easy to get caught up in what feels good to you, but don't forget about them, including their orgasm.

Don't judge them or make them feel self-conscious about what turns them on or what they do. There is nothing more unattractive than being made to feel guilty or ashamed of what instinctively turns them on. You wouldn't want them to do that to you, so you shouldn't do that to them.

Action Plan for "Be Enticing" quality

Take their preferences into consideration when it comes to showing passion for, and attracting, them.

Visual connection using a team approach:

- ⊙ Have empathy for connection they feel with their eyes.
- ⊙ Take their visual preferences into consideration.

Don't put more effort for others than your spouse:

- ⊙ Put similar effort at home as much as at work or going out.
- ⊙ Balance being comfortable with what they prefer.

Flirty and seductive:

- ⊙ Use flirty, charming words and provocative, sexy actions.
- ⊙ Use innocent yet suggestive touching.

Bond through sexual connection:

- ⊙ Have sexual variety and take turns on preferences.
- ⊙ See sex as connection fulfillment and tension release.

Chapter 11

Team Quality #5

Be Affectionate

Spend Time Together

This was one of the things Abby most looked forward to. Weekends meant spending time with Travis. It was a time that was extremely important to her because just being around each other was joyful to her, which Travis needed to remember. She enjoyed his company and doing things with him. She didn't need elaborate plans or activities to do. Even just hanging around the house was something she loved to do with him.

Spending time together with your spouse can be done in very simple ways. This is both going out on dates and just spending casual time together at home, enjoying each other's company. Don't let being married stop you from going out on dates together and doing something you both enjoy.

You don't have to spend money doing this. Go on a walk with your spouse, go out to a cheap movie or run errands together. Research things to do that are free or inexpensive. There are multiple things to do without spending much money, but you do have to do a little research to find them. Most of the things you do together can be very simple, rather than elaborate plans.

Simple doesn't mean it's boring and doesn't mean they take it for granted. Focus on things that your spouse enjoys doing, but it doesn't have to exclusively be things that only they enjoy. They just enjoy spending time with you, even if it means also doing things that you enjoy.

Time apart with friends and hobbies is important, but be careful not to overdo it. It may mean a lot to them to have a set routine of doing certain things together, such as having coffee in the morning together to start the day or going to bed together.

Give what you're doing with your spouse your complete attention at times, even just at home. It's easy to get distracted with other things when you're supposed to be enjoying each other's company and time together. For example, if you're watching a movie together or playing a game, put away other distractions and give them your exclusive focus.

One of the ways to spend time together is to do a shared activity together. It can be an interest that they have, you have or a new activity that you're both trying out. Either physically participate with them or even just watch them do it. These can be things like cooking together, doing a home improvement project or doing some kind of art/craft activity.

When you spend time together in social situations, observe the situation you're in and adapt your actions and behavior accordingly. Our life is made up of many different situations that we're in. Being a complex person means that you are able to distinguish between those situations and act accordingly. You're not being fake when you let your actions and behavior adjust to whatever situation you're in at the time.

It's easy to display child-like behaviors rather than adult-like behaviors when you're comfortable with someone. Just remember that your spouse wants to spend time with you as an adult, not a child. If they see juvenile or child-like behaviors from you, it's harder for them to make the transition to seeing you as an adult when you're trying to be romantic with them.

There is a difference between being playful and being overly goofy. Too much of one can be okay for your spouse, while too much of the other can be an irritation to them. Some spouses will like one type over the other. You have to watch for clues on what your spouse likes and what is turning them off.

Don't Over-Focus on Other Things

"I've been busy all day with other things, it's his turn now," she smiled to herself. Life was busy. There was work, the kids' activities, hobbies, family obligations. Emily knew her time and attention were stretched thin. But she knew it was important to Frank that she take time just for him. He wasn't selfish. He didn't want all of her time. He just wanted to feel as important to her as the other stuff going on in her life. Once she found little ways to do this, it became quite easy and not time consuming.

Your spouse admires that you are a good parent, a hard worker and are intelligent, but they can often feel that they are only a very small part of your life. They can feel taken for granted when you think everything is okay between you two only after things on your to-do list are completed. They want to know you are thinking about them when you do things for them or with them.

It may be the little things they are seeking regarding attention. They could be just looking for little acknowledgments from you that you are thinking about them and that they are just as important as the things on your do-do list. They're simply looking for some small amounts of attention given to them when you've been busy giving your attention elsewhere.

Emily had been hugging the kids when she paused a moment to give Frank a quick hug. This was often all he needed from her. Just a quick acknowledgment that he's there and just as important as the kids. She does the same thing with compliments.

If you just visited your family for a holiday or dinner, offer to go visit their family next. If you've been busy with errands all day or visiting a friend, offer to watch their favorite program with them that night.

Just look at ways to satisfy both your own to-do list and their need for a little attention, rather than just assuming everything is okay when you say no to something they request because you have other things to do.

Your spouse wants to know you're thinking about them when you're not physically together. Sending a message to them during the day is a great way to do it. It can be as simple as "I hope you're having a great day" or relaying something funny about your day. Remind them why you love them and why they are so special to you.

They may appreciate having the periodic reminders more than they can ever express to you. Romance to them is often not the big over-the-top gestures. It's the simple little things that are ways to show them that you're thinking about them and appreciate that they are in your life.

When life is busy, give your spouse a specific time when you can meet their desires. The main thing they want to know is that you understand how important something is to them and you don't take it lightly or brush it aside. You want to please them and do what's important to them, but you just can't at the moment. Just be careful not to put it off too long or too many times.

They understand their needs may take a backseat for a little while, but eventually they will get frustrated and refuse to meet your needs out of frustration. Days can then quickly turn into weeks, months and years of unmet needs for both of you. Know that you must focus on your efforts toward them during certain times in life. It may seem natural and normal to start to waiver on meeting their requests when big things happen in your life.

For example, when you have a baby as a couple. The natural thing is to focus on the baby. After all, a baby needs lots of attention and care, and you are more tired than you were before with suddenly very little time for yourself.

You may feel that life will slow down at some point in the future and you will be able to get back to putting some focus on your spouse again. But then you realize that a two-year-old toddler takes just as much time and energy as when the baby is a month old or a year old. By then you two may be ready to have another baby, which starts the cycle all over again. Before you know it, several years down the road and two kids later neither of you have been doing what's important to the other one for a very long time.

You may give time and attention to the baby that you used to give to your spouse. They understand this is natural, but they can still feel hurt, ignored and unloved. They may react by spending less time at home, less time helping around the house and less time meeting your desires. Then it would be your turn to feel hurt, ignored and unloved.

You may react to this by spending even more time and attention on your child and getting frustrated that your spouse isn't around more to help.

Once this cycle begins, it is hard to get out of it. For years it can continue for both of you. Realize that you may both be at fault and both contribute to this downward spiral. Remember that although the baby needs time and attention, don't forget that your spouse also needs time, attention and reassurances too.

One way you can avoid this kind of problem is by giving them a specific time, in the very near future, when you can fulfill what's important to them. They are much more likely to be accepting of a refusal if they know when they will be getting that need met soon.

Affectionate Touching

"Brr!" Lilly's feet felt cold next to his, but Gordon didn't mind. One of her favorite things to do was to lay on the couch with him watching a movie and let her bare feet be warmed by his. This simple little act made her feel as close to him as anything else. Knowing this, how could he possibly deny her this one little quirk!

Giving physical affection is giving your spouse a little piece of you. You are conveying that they are worth that physical piece of yourself. Showing physical nourishment to them is as important as giving emotional nourishment to them.

Give your spouse affection such as kissing, cuddling, hugging and hand holding. Sometimes you need to be the one to initiate the kiss hello and goodbye, the hug while walking past your spouse, the cuddle on the couch together. They want to feel you are coming after them for these things, even when they may be the one who wants it more than you do.

Some of the best ways to show affection are everyday things like putting your hand on their knee sitting next to them at dinner. Or brushing their back as you pass by them in the kitchen. Let them touch you without making a comment or acting aggravated about it. The normal, every day physical touch can be just as important to your spouse as other ways of feeling connected.

You can greet them enthusiastically when either of you come home, rather than grunting at them or worse yet, not even acknowledging them. Make them feel cherished and that you are happy to be near them. The same goes for when either of you leave the home.

Don't get complacent in showing affection to them or get too overly comfortable with them. It's easy to go days, weeks or even months without much affection between you. Being too comfortable can make you exhibit certain actions and behaviors that your spouse finds irritating or unattractive.

Don't get aggravated when they show physical affection to you, even if you're busy doing something else at the moment. It's easy to focus on what you're doing and not want to be disturbed while you're doing it. But remember, this could be a vital way they feel connected to you and will give back to you in the ways you feel connected to them.

Physical affection is also habit forming. The more you do it, the easier it is to do it without even thinking about it. It just becomes automatic. In the other direction, it becomes automatic to not do it when you repeatedly don't do it.

Watch Out For Their Well-Being

She didn't realize how much it affected him, but now she felt awful. It was easy for Danielle to make fun of Isaac's unique traits that felt foreign to her. She figured he had thick skin and he shouldn't be bothered by it. But she was wrong. He was bothered by it on an emotional level. They trusted each other to watch out for each other's physical well-being, but they also needed to be just as careful about being cognizant of their emotional well-being too.

One way to show affection toward your spouse is to watch out for their physical health and well-being. Without being overbearing about it, keep an eye out for dangers and to make sure they feel safe physically. You can do this in a subtle and discreet manner, so you don't make it out to be too over-protective.

If they're sick or injured, pay extra attention to them to help them. They can feel especially in need of safety because they don't feel good. This is when they can really appreciate you giving them a little extra care, attention and affection.

In the same manner, watch out for their emotional well-being by being careful of making teasing or mocking comments to them or about them. Your spouse may not have the same sense of humor you do, so even sassy, sarcastic or joking comments can be hurtful or irritating.

Be aware of little, innocuous statements you make. Sometimes you may say something without thinking how it will affect them, even if you're trying to be funny. This can happen more easily if they are already self-conscious about something.

This may occur when you go along with what other people joke about. What friends or other people may think is humorous or general entertainment, may not be funny to your spouse and can actually be insensitive and hurtful to them. Put yourself in their shoes and think how you would feel about certain things about you being mocked.

You may be just trying to show that you're a funny person or trying to make a story more interesting to other people. But that's not always a good way to do it. You are placing more emphasis on how other people are viewing you at that moment than watching out for your spouse's emotional well-being.

It can create a big divide with your spouse. You can start to actually view them in the way you're making a joke of. Just as bad, they can also start to believe it about themselves, which isn't good for their self-esteem.

Joking too much can also make them feel like more of a sibling to you than an intimate spouse. You may be able to get away with saying or doing things with your sibling or a good friend that would make your spouse feel uncomfortable. Remember that there is a difference between the two.

When speaking with your spouse, having conversations about other people can be normal. But be careful when making comments about other people to your spouse. Your spouse wants to feel unique and special to you. So even well-meaning comments about the appearance of another person can be taken the wrong way by your spouse.

In addition, if you stare at or flirt with other people, they don't feel unique to you. Even an innocent comment with someone else can send the wrong message to them about your intentions. It's okay to appreciate the qualities of another person but be careful how your words or actions can affect your spouse.

Unappealing Habits and Remember Dating Days

One of the biggest lessons Kennedy and Taylor learned in marriage was to look at each other's perspective. It was easy for them to focus on what they want out of the marriage. But what made their marriage great was realizing that each of them wants something different in the marriage and the way to promote happiness is to make an effort to give that to each other. Doing what they wouldn't normally do was hard, but essential.

You can make your spouse feel cherished and not taken for granted by showing your interest in them. Taking them for granted can come about in two ways. One, being overly comfortable around them by doing things that are unappealing to them. Two, saying no to their desires and still expecting them to be happy, unlike what you would do in your early dating days together.

Showing your spouse they can depend on you and rely on you is a good way to show you're not being overly comfortable around them. This includes listening to them about how comfortable they are with your use of alcohol, drugs, financial spending, etc. It can include honoring time commitments, being on time for things with them and careful about how much time you spend on activities not involving your spouse.

Also think about any other habits you have that might not be very appealing to your spouse. Things you wouldn't do during the early dating days when you're trying to impress them. Think about how they view you when you do certain things. You want to be comfortable around them, but you don't want to be a turn off around them either.

Realize that you may be doing things that are a turn off to them. While you want to be yourself, think about how their desire toward you might be affected by your actions and behavior. Don't be someone you're not, but don't be actively unattractive to your spouse either.

Remembering your dating days is also good for stopping yourself from saying no to their desires and still expecting them to be happy. This was the time when you didn't worry about being happy with the thing they requested to be done. Instead, you simply focused on the happiness of your new dating partner. You weren't worried about being happy with the thing requested, only with the happiness that thing brought to them.

Remember back to those days and remind yourself that your goal is not to be happy about the thing they are requesting now. Your goal is to see the happiness it brings to them when it's fulfilled and to do it for them in a good way.

Sometimes your pleasure shouldn't only come from you feeling good about what you want to do for them or give to them. It has to also come from making them feel good in the specific way they need it from you. It's not about grinning and bearing it. It's about doing things for each other that truly make the other one happy, as long as pain or going against values isn't involved.

Realize that when they make a request to you, you really have two options. Option A is to meet the request and ensure they will be happy when it's met. They will be fulfilled in the marriage and more likely to meet your request of them later on.

Option B is to not meet the request because you don't feel like it or don't want to take the time at that moment. But along with option B is knowing and accepting that they will be unhappy and frustrated with the marriage and less likely to do what's important to you later on.

Like a lot of people, you probably want there to be an option C. Option C is ignoring or denying their request, yet still expecting them to be completely happy, satisfied in the marriage and continue to do what's important to you. But there is no option C. They make the request because it's important to them, plays a factor in their happiness in the marriage and motivates them to fulfill your desires.

You may think saying no to their desires does not affect their happiness. But life doesn't work that way. Where a marriage may have problems is when you believe that you should individually follow your own happiness and that your own actions and decisions do not affect the happiness of your spouse. Individuality is important, but not at the expense of your spouse.

If your spouse is not feeling connected in the marriage because you have denied the things that help build that connection for them, how can you expect them to fulfill the things that build a connection for you? The marriage itself needs a connection from both sides. Making sacrifices for each other is okay and needed sometimes for the health of the marriage.

You have every right to say no to something they want, but doing this repeatedly will rarely help a marriage be fulfilling for either one of you. Neither of you will be inspired to go outside your comfort zone for the other one when they hear no on the things most important to them.

Expanding your comfort zone may be a key factor. Remember that you don't have to love the thing that your spouse is requesting. You just have to love the happiness and fulfillment that thing brings to them. It's okay to do something that's purely for their pleasure. They are more inspired to fulfill your desires when they are happy.

Action Plan for "Be Affectionate" quality

Give them direct, focused affection, attention and equal priority with other things in your life.

Spend time together:

- ⊙ Spend time with each other on dates and relaxing at home.
- ⊙ Give what you're doing with them your complete attention.

Don't over-focus on other things:

- ⊙ Make them feel as important to you as other things.
- ⊙ Give a specific time when you can meet their needs.

Affectionate touching:

- ⊙ Give physical affection with kissing, cuddling, hugging.
- ⊙ Do little things such as casual physical contact.

Watch out for their well-being:

- ⊙ Make them feel safe physically with an eye out for danger.
- ⊙ Watch out for their emotional well-being; limit teasing.

Unappealing habits and remember dating days:

- ⊙ Think about their comfort level with your habits.
- ⊙ Make them feel cherished, not taken for granted.

Section Four

The "Inspire" Challenge

Key Advice - Listen to, and do, what's important to each other because a spouse's actions, behavior and words can either pull the other spouse closer or push them away.

Inspire each other — Consistently perform actions that fulfill each other's top Independent and Team quality that each of you find most appealing. When someone displays a quality their spouse finds appealing, the spouse can be inspired to reciprocate.

Inspire your spouse — The ideal is to display these qualities to each other, but you may have to be the one to display it first to inspire them to also do what's important to you. Even if you have to guess at what their two top qualities are.

Inspire yourself — Focus your efforts on these two qualities they find most attractive. But the more of the other qualities you put effort to, the better the marriage can be and more well-rounded you can be as a person.

Chapter 12

Dealing With Issues

Running Into Problems

"I don't like your actions," Reese said. "Well I don't like your behavior," Payton returned. Both were willing to point out what the other one was doing wrong, but neither was willing to admit that their own actions and behavior were unappealing and contributing to the problem.

When a problem arises, go back to the basic tenants of this book's concept. First, put equal focus on both the Independent quality and Team quality parts. It can be easy to over-emphasize doing one type more than the other. But it's vital to give both types of qualities the same effort, during the good times and tough times.

Second, treat each other's perspective equally, regarding what each of you desire. If you want them to display the qualities you desire and are important to you, don't dismiss, judge or ridicule the qualities they desire and important to them; and vice versa. Remember, you're trying to create a positive feedback loop, not a negative one.

Finally, think about your attitude when displaying those qualities. Are you grumbling about doing it, instead of doing it with a smile on your face? Do those things because you genuinely want to do what's important to your spouse, not because you feel you have to.

When you feel distance, tension or a problem in the marriage, think about which qualities either of you could be missing from the other. Ask yourself two questions. What could my spouse do differently to do what's important to me or that I have a strong attraction to? What could I do differently to do what's important to them or that they have a strong attraction to?

When you don't like an action or behavior of theirs, having a direct conversation about it is a good first step. But sometimes there is a reason why someone does something, even if they don't realize it themselves. So even if they change, it could be short-lived. If it is short-lived, take a different approach as a second step.

Could their actions or behavior be an instinctive reaction to your actions or behavior? You may be able to inspire their change by changing what you do. Remember, this is *Inspire Your Marriage*, which means you get them to fulfill your desires by fulfilling their desires. Direct communication is not a bad thing to do, but it shouldn't be the only thing you do to fix problems in the marriage.

Keep in mind that what is attractive to us today may change over time. So it's a good idea to re-take the quiz when you have a major life event, such as having a baby; or when the marriage is going through a rough time, even though you think you're both doing the things each other finds most important.

In addition to each of your two top qualities, think about other areas each of you find attractive. Either of you may not find an overall quality attractive, but do find one section within in it to be very attractive. Put a little effort into that section as well.

Also remember that your marriage is only yours and your spouse's. You have a right to mold your marriage the way you and your spouse want it to be, not what friends, family or others think it should be like. Don't think your marriage needs to imitate what you read, hear or see elsewhere. Definitely don't feel guilt about how both of you want it to be.

Pitfalls to Each Type of Quality

Don't use the Independent qualities to act single or try to have the benefits of being single and being married. Being married doesn't mean you give up independence, but it does mean you give up being single. You can be single or you can be married. You can't be both and you can't have the benefits of both.

The opposite problem people run into when trying to show an Independent quality to their spouse is they overly focus on their spouse's happiness when doing it, ignoring their own happiness. That's not showing an Independent quality, it's showing a Team quality and can border on being a doormat.

For the Team qualities, don't dictate what your spouse must do or try to cut them off from their friends and family, insinuating you have to be a team apart from everyone else. A team puts the best interests of their partner as an important priority, unless what they desire goes against your values or morals.

A different problem people run into when trying to show a Team quality to their spouse is giving that quality in the way they want to give it or when they want to give it, not how their spouse finds it most attractive. That's not showing a Team quality, it's showing an Independent quality and can border on being selfish.

Try it as a Solo Experiment

What if your spouse isn't on board to do this with you? As an experiment, do it by yourself. Again, there's a reason it's called *Inspire Your Marriage*. If you do the things that make them happy, it may get them to do things that make you happy.

A healthy marriage is about displaying those qualities to each other, but you may have to be the one to display it first. When you display a quality they find appealing, they may be inspired to reciprocate back to you of what you find appealing.

Another option if they won't read the book, but seem open to the general concept, is to show them the Action Plan of the two qualities that mean the most to you. Some people simply are not readers and would be difficult to sit down long enough to read a book, but are willing to do certain actions that are easy to digest and laid out for them so they can understand it.

Either way, give it time to work, especially if you're in a long-time relationship. The longer you've been together, the more time is needed. If you've been together for a while, it may take longer for them to see the changes and be assured it won't be a short term, temporary or inconsistent thing on your part.

One thing that may help is if a friend takes the quiz too, discuss your quiz answers with them. Note this is not a gripe session about what your spouse is not doing. It's about helping each other give insight on how to inspire each of your spouses to make the marriages better, as well as what self-improvement you're seeing. But remember, each marriage is different, so no judgment about someone else's style of marriage.

A lot of this can be considered self-improvement. You can see benefits for yourself as well as for the marriage. Just doing something different might make you feel better about yourself, which is always worthwhile.

Inspire Someone Else's Marriage

Like what you see here and thinking about what you can do to help other marriages? Here are a few ways you can help someone else's marriage be a little stronger:

1. Buy a copy of this book to give as a present.
2. Post a positive review on a book selling website.
3. Recommend it on your social media page or an online message board forum.
4. Give away copies of this book as a marketing tool for your business.

Section Five

The Attraction Quiz

The following "Independent and Team Qualities Quiz" will give insight into which Independent quality and which Team quality you are most attracted to when your spouse displays them. If your spouse also takes it, it will show the qualities they are most attracted to when you display them.

The quiz has two sections. Part 1 is identifying the Independent qualities and Part 2 is identifying the Team qualities.

If your spouse won't take the quiz, you can take it for them and guess at how you think they would answer each question. Fill it out based on how they have reacted to things in the past.

Independent and Team Qualities Quiz

Part 1

Which Independent Quality Do You Find Most Attractive?

For each number below, choose one of the two options that you find slightly more appealing when your spouse does it.

The two options have a letter, A to E, representing one of the five main types of Independent qualities. These five types will be identified at the end of the quiz.

Example – for number 1, choose either A or B; for number 2, choose either D or E; and so on.

I find it more appealing when my spouse:
(choose one of the two options, mark your selections)

1. A. Knows how to take care of things, including household, kids.
   B. Is passionate about something in life.

2. D. Does exciting things to live in the moment.
   E. Doesn't need my attention to feel content.

3. C. Is bold and direct about things.
   D. Focuses on fun and enjoyment in life.

4. A. Is adept at handling semi-common tasks.

    C. Is assertive when they want something.

5. B. Shows an interesting side with interests, hobbies, friends.

    E. Doesn't try too hard to get my attention too often.

6. A. Knows what to do and has a plan for activities, events.

    E. Backs off a little so I can show my interest to them.

7. B. Shows they're good or impressive at something.

    D. Breaks from normal routine to be carefree.

8. A. Doesn't mirror or try to fix my mood.

    D. Is engaging and talkative with people.

9. B. Continually expands their knowledge and learning.

    C. Makes decisions when asked or needed, not indecisive.

10. C. Isn't always giving in to my desires and thoughts.

    E. Gives space and time apart occasionally.

11. A. Doesn't let my words or emotions affect them negatively.

    B. Challenges themselves to overcome obstacles, even own flaws.

12. D. Uses banter and humor to build chemistry.

    E. Doesn't feel a need to be around each other constantly.

13. C. Believes in themselves and their abilities.

    D. Has a vibrant, lively side to them.

14. A. Doesn't act different or analyze my mood when I'm quiet.

    C. Stands up for their morals and values, even with me.

15. B. Is dedicated to an active, healthy lifestyle.

    E. Doesn't feel they always have to impress or do things for me.

16. A. Leads their life controlling their finances, alcohol, drugs.

    E. Waits for me to initiate contact verbally, physically sometimes.

17. B. Shows ambition, drive and goals in life.

    D. Creates a playful spark outside the bedroom.

18. A. Doesn't need excessive assistance in life in general.

    D. Shows sexual ravishment toward me, with my consent.

19. B. Puts effort into visual presence, grooming, hygiene.

    C. Is self-assured regardless of the situation they're in.

20. C. Shows strength to lead through issues in life.

    E. Lets me do things for them or asks me for a favor at times.

Results

Go back and add up the number of times you selected each letter in this quiz part 1 section. The letters represent the Independent quality of being:

A = Self-Reliant

B = Personal Development Focused

C = Confident

D = Full of Life

E = Self-Fulfilling

The letter with the highest number of times selected means that you are most attracted to that quality when your spouse displays it. The maximum score for each letter is 8.

Score of 6-8 = highly appealing quality to you

Score of 4-5 = moderately appealing quality to you

Score of 0-3 = lower appealing quality to you

Which Independent quality do you find most attractive?

Independent and Team Qualities Quiz

Part 2

Which Team Quality Do You Find Most Attractive?

For each number below, choose one of the two options that you find slightly more appealing when your spouse does it.

The two options have a letter, A to E, representing one of the five main types of Team qualities. These five types will be identified at the end of the quiz.

Example – for number 1, choose either A or B; for number 2, choose either D or E; and so on.

I find it more appealing when my spouse:

(choose one of the two options, mark your selections)

1. A. Supports me by letting me express my feelings.
    B. Smiles and shows their warm, pleasant side often.

2. D. Is subtly seductive with charm and flirting.
    E. Spends time with me, including going out.

3. C. Lets small things go, not easily upset or complaining.
    D. Thinks about what I would enjoy visually about them.

4. A. Listens to me vent and get things off my chest.

    C. Isn't nit-picking or contradicting me often.

5. B. Builds me up and doesn't bad mouth others.

    E. Gives affection with kissing, hand holding, etc.

6. A. Has conversations often with me.

    E. Touches me randomly during the day.

7. B. Says happy, positive things more than negativity.

    D. Is willing to try new things sexually as variety.

8. A. Does household chores with a thought to how I like it.

    D. Puts similar effort into their appearance at home as going out.

9. B. Shows enthusiasm when doing activities together.

    C. Doesn't appear combative or trying to be "right".

10. C. Isn't rigid about things being their way.

    E. Shows interest in me, making me feel cherished.

11. A. Compromises or takes turns doing activities each other likes.

    B. Has a kind, positive energy and an uplifting presence.

12. D. Touches me in a casual, but very suggestive way.

    E. Gives and wants attention without teasing comments.

13. C. Is easy going and relaxed in life.

    D. Puts out intentional effort to attract me.

14. A. Knows what they can do to help me and be supportive.

    C. Gives me benefit of doubt to assume my intentions are good.

15. B. Shows appreciation, encouragement and empathy.

    E. Gives me as much attention as other things in their life.

16. A. Talks about subject I enjoy without it being about them.

    E. Is watchful of my physical well-being and safety.

17. B. Believes in me, even when I make a mistake.

    D. Balances their physical comfort with my visual preferences.

18. A. Does thoughtful acts, such as remembering foods I like.

    D. Sees sex as one way to connect and truly shows desire.

19. B. Asks nicely for things, not a demanding order.

    C. Doesn't give too much advice or try to control things.

20. C. Handles frustration well without a temper or over-reacting.

    E. Spends casual quiet time with me, even just at home.

Results

Go back and add up the number of times you selected each letter in this quiz part 2 section. The letters represent the Team quality of being:

A = Supportive

B = Uplifting

C = Easy Going

D = Enticing

E = Affectionate

The letter with the highest number of times selected means that you are most attracted to that quality when your spouse displays it. The maximum score for each letter is 8.

Score of 6-8 = highly appealing quality to you

Score of 4-5 = moderately appealing quality to you

Score of 0-3 = lower appealing quality to you

Which Team quality do you find most attractive?

The 5 Independent Qualities

Here is the outline of each of the five Independent qualities. You will feel more of a connection with your spouse when they display the quality you find most desirable from the quiz.

1) Self-reliant – This quality is when your spouse doesn't need excessive assistance in life and doesn't get thrown off course emotionally.

2) Personal development focused – This quality is when your spouse is interesting through their own personal development and determination in life.

3) Confident – This quality is when your spouse shows they're self-assured regardless of the situation they're in and bold about things in life.

4) Full of life – This quality is when your spouse shows their fun side of being carefree and letting loose.

5) Self-fulfilling – This quality is when your spouse doesn't need your attention or approval for how fulfilled and content they are in life.

The 5 Team Qualities

Here is the outline of each of the five Team qualities. You will feel more of a connection with your spouse when they display the quality you find most desirable from the quiz.

1) Supportive – This quality is when your spouse does things as a way to be helpful, caring and support you.

2) Uplifting – This quality is when your spouse has a kind, positive energy about them and lifts you up with a good-natured attitude.

3) Easy going – This quality is when your spouse is easy going and relaxed in life, especially towards you.

4) Enticing – This quality is when your spouse takes your preferences into consideration when it comes to showing passion for, and attracting, you.

5) Affectionate – This quality is when your spouse gives you direct, focused affection, attention and equal priority with other things in their life.

<u>Reminder of Main Concept / Advice</u>

Listen to, and do, what's important to each other because a spouse's actions, behavior and words can either pull the other spouse closer or push them away. Your actions create reactions in your spouse.

Inspire Your Marriage

www.InspireYourMarriage.com

Made in the USA
Las Vegas, NV
24 December 2021

39334597R00115